The Goddess Blackwoman

Mother of Civilization

International Standard Book Number
#1-56411-129-6

Manufactured in the United States of America
First Draft Edition 1992
Second Revised Draft Edition 1994

Final Revised Edition August 1995
Second Printing-Final Revised Edition June 1996
Third Printing-Final Revised Edition November 1996

12 Lessons to Restore The Image, The Character, & The Responsibility of The Goddess Blackwoman
(Spirituality/Self Development $12.95)

Published By
Nia Communications/Press
P.O.B. 5631 • St. Louis, MO • 63121

Note to the Reader:

How to Read This Book from Beginning to End?

In a world that makes it increasingly difficult for us to find the time to read, I offer this suggestion.

Make an agreement to yourself to read *"one section per-day"*, possibly in the evening before you fall asleep. There are *"12 Lessons"* in addition to the *"3 Lessons of Part One"*. This works out to be just about *"One Lesson per day"* for two weeks.

After that first review, come back to re-read the lessons for reinforcement, and also to make sure that you recieve the whole of the message. The meaning of the words will change, grow, and deepen, upon each time that you read them over. This is because, "you" will change, grow, and deepen, as your understanding evolves stage by stage.

Let this be one book, that you read from beggining to end, and over again. This is a workshop, a workbook, and a study guide. This is not entertainment, fiction, or a storybook. This is a "study guide" to be continuously reviewed, re-read, studied, and referred to for daily growth, instruction, guidance, and improvement. This is a "hand-book", so keep this book "on hand" wherever you go. Okay? Okay.

Thank you, and I hope you enjoy the reading. See you at the end of the book.

Table Of Contents

Subject Directory

Introduction:
The Restoration of The Goddess Blackwoman
"Re-civilizing The Mother of Civilization"

Preface:
You are Much More than You Think
"The Goddess By Nature"

•••••

Part I Divine Purpose & Responsibility
"The Mission, The Why, & The How"

Part II Divine Image & Character
12 Points of Character Cleansing
"Do We Still Do the things that We Used to?"

Introduction:

The Restoration of The Goddess Blackwoman

"Re-civilizing The Mother of Civilization"

It is with the most sincere, adoration, love, honor, and respect, that I humbly submit these writings to you, Blackwoman.

I submit this message because it has been all too often in this "temporary", but "transitory", evil world, that the Blackwoman is looked over, devalued, discarded, and disrespected. I know that this world has forgotten to honor thy Mother, The Original Blackwoman. But yet what is even more tragic, is that this Original Blackwoman has forgotten to honor her own self.

This world has dishonored and disrespected her for so long, that she has now learned to dishonor and disrespect her own self! She is now left as a "Queen with no Queendom", and a "Goddess with no Glory". The "Mother of Civilization", now living in a most "uncivilized state". Imagine that. No, just look around at that fact.

This is so sad. And this is so true. But wait, this is going to be no sad story. So, dry your eyes today. The title of this message is called "Re-Storing...Re-storing...Re-storing The Image, The Character, & The Responsibility of The Goddess Blackwoman". This is the Re-building!...the Restoration!...the Re-construction!

Understand that yesterday is over, and today is right now! So, dry your eyes. In case you haven't heard, this Blackwoman today is on a mission! She is on a powerfully divine mission to restore "her own self-honor" and "her own self-respect" first, which will prepare her to once again restore "honor" and "respect" throughout the world! This is what it means to righteously re-assert herself as The Original Queen Mother of Civilization to an entire World, that has gone astray! Can you hear this?

Oh, I hope you can hear this. Just keep reading, you'll begin to remember. It will all eventually come back to you...just keep going. Keep going.

See, today is that predicted day, when the True, Real, Living, Blackwoman of Righteousness, is to rise up from the deathly grave of self-ignorance, back up into the illuminated sphere of Supreme Wisdom. In fact, today is that day when she is to once again "become" that illuminated sphere of Supreme Wisdom. You shall become this "again". This is that day. Think over that. Think deeply over that.

So no, this is no sad story. No, this is no sad story...no, not anymore...because you have picked up this book for a definite Reason and a definite Purpose. You have picked up this book seeking to Improve the Condition of Your Self, and Your Life. And, when you Sincerely Seek to find that which is Good for you, then that which is Good for you, shall Always Seek to find You. That is the Law.

To seek "Good", is to seek "God". So, **as long as you are sincerely seeking and reaching for that which is higher than yourself, your rise is perpetually guaranteed and inevitable.**

You are Rising as we speak. You are Rising as you Reach! And it is "Your Rise" that will "Raise All" that have received life through you. You are just going to have to stop and think about that right there.

•••••

I must fully stress again that it is <u>your</u> blessed

"womb of wisdom", that is to rise again to give life and re-birth to your newborn budding Black Nation...your Womb is your Mind, dear sister. Think about these words. And this newborn Black Nation shall suckle at the life-sustaining milk, of The Most Supreme Wisdom...this Milk is your Thoughts, dear sister.

It is "Your Nation" which will suckle at The Milk of this Divine Flow of Thinking, that we all may be Nurtured, Grown, Restored, and Rejuvenated into a healthy state of mental, physical, and spiritual maturity once again. This is that time! This is "Your" time. And because of that, this is "Our" time. You, birth, feed, and nurture The Entire Nation. It's true. You are much more important than what you think you are.

This is exactly why you have to deeply get to know your own self all over again, as a Blackwoman, even if everyone else is not ready to know who and what you truly are. You need to know you! You know you first! And the rest of the world will just have to get prepared and ready to eventually get acquainted with you too.

Although, first things first, **"you"** must know **"you"**, in order to properly know **"who"** you are supposed to be, **"what"** you are supposed to do, and **"how"** you are supposed to do it.

Without this central "Knowledge of Self", you will be lost and left to blow wherever the winds of this misguided corrupted society takes you...just imitating your atmosphere...following the blind foolishness of the blind fools. But, we don't want that. No, we do not want that anymore.

•••••

So, if it be the will of Almighty God Allah, I pray that these writings may "assist" you in that re-introduction of yourself, to yourself...your Real Self, your Truest Self, your Goddess Self.

Introduction

Get ready to meet the real you, because you are not who "they" say you are! You are no second-class citizen! You are no unimportant, worthless, inferior, human being! You are much more than who and what "they" say you are!

If there were no "You", there would be no "They"...or no "Us". They don't understand that you are the doorway through which all Creation has come itself. Wait now. I said, "you are the doorway through which all Creation has come itself." That is something to think over for a while. And if "they" don't understand that right now, so what? You just make sure that "you" understand that right now, for your own self. Okay? Okay.

Listen now. All of this has been said to say that, as a Blackwoman, you have got some work to do...you have got some duties to complete today. You have got some household cleaning duties to attend to. Yes...and you better realize that your household spans from one side of the planet to the other! That is what it means to be the Mother of Entire Civilization itself. This is no small thing. Do you understand what's being said to you?

Well, these writings are designed to help you prepare for that great work and duty of putting your entire household back in order. And you prepare to get your Universal household in order, by first getting your own personal self in order.

This is designed to assist and inspire "The Mother of Civilization" at re-civilizing her own self, up and out of the uncivilized conditioned that this world has cast her down into. That is the purpose of this conversation!

Now, where is that Mighty Goddess Blackwoman? There you are right there! She was lost, but now she is found. So, come on home to re-claim the high-esteem of your throne...being courageous enough to accept what is truly your own...courageous enough to be that which is truly yourself...taking your life back!

Peace.

Preface

You are Much More than You Think

"The Goddess By Nature"

I don't care where you are in your life right now Blackwoman. I don't care at what level in this society you may currently be, but you have already been declared a "Goddess" by nature. Are you listening? "You" have already been declared a divine "Goddess" by nature...a "Goddess"!

You are already an heir to the Throne, and the legacy of Divine Ancient Royalty is in the very blood that courses through your very veins, at this very moment. Yes, and I am still talking to "You". "You" right there. Yes, "You"! But you don't hear this, do you? You don't know what this means, do you? No, you don't hear this.

See, regardless to who and what you may think yourself to be, "you" have automatically been declared a "Queen Goddess Blackwoman", simply from your birthright. "The Mother of Civilization"! This is your true nature! But you still don't know what this means, do you? Do you?

No, you don't know this truth about yourself, because, in this society, you have had no one to teach you of who and what you "truly" are. So, how could you know? You have not really known your own "Self-Identity". No one has taught you a true "Knowledge of your Divine Self". No, you have not known you.

And a Goddess, who does not consciously know that she is a "Goddess", is just as good as not being a Goddess at all! A Blackwoman, who does not consciously know that she is "The Mother of Civilization", will become the epitome of an "uncivilized" woman herself! Right?

As we have said, with no knowledge of her true self, she will just imitate her atmosphere...being an impostor Blackwoman. Imitating the low-charactered image that her oppressor has directed her to imitate. We witness this to be true everyday.

•••••

No, I'm sorry, you just have not known you...and you can only be, what it is that you know. So, what do you know? What do you know Blackwoman? The shameful truth is that, you only know that, which those who have mastered you, have taught you to know! That is a shame sister. That is just a shame, but that is the truth.

Here you are, still existing as the "lowly cattepillar", who has never been told that you actually were a "Butterfly" in disguise? So, of course, you have never tried to fly. You have never even thought to make that transformation. You thought that it was your natural place, to crawl around, in the low-levels of this world for the rest of your life. But, it is not so.

Being lied to all the days of this life, as a Blackwoman, while not knowing "who" and "what" you actually were, has left you to be a Mis-guided Goddess...making you function and behave as something less than what your nature truly is.

Yes, you are a Misguided Goddess, but still a Goddess! A "Sleeping Goddess"! Asleep and unconscious to the Potential Greatness of your own individual soul! Deceived out of your own destiny! No, I'm sorry, but you just don't know who and what you truly are.

See, it is only logical that when you are unaware of the "internal contents" of your own being, that you would not and could not know your own "life purpose" and/or "destiny in life". If you don't know "what you are", you don't know "what to be". And since this world has taught me that I am cheap, worthless, and inferior...I'll be cheap, worthless, and inferior. You are what you have been made to think that you are.

•••••

The bottom-line lesson that this truth teaches us is this: *"It is only a Knowledgeable Awareness of The True Contents of Self, which will activate Those Contents of Self, into Self-Expression.*

If one is not aware of the Potentiality of Greatness that rests within themselves, they will never Willfully Demand that this Greatness be Awakened and Arisen into expression."

But today, you are going to be made aware of the True Contents of Yourself. You are going to be informed of your True Identity. Today you are going to re-discover who you are "in" this world, and what you are "to" this world. You will have a Knowledgeable Awareness of the Contents of Self.

You are definitely "much more" than what you "think" you are, beloved Blackwoman. And, in order to Survive as well as Succeed in This Life, you had better know this today!

For your Own Sake, it is time to re-awaken into the remembrance of your Own Self, and return home unto the sanity of your Own Mind...your Right Mind...your Righteous Mind...your Goddess Mind. If you do not do this right here and now, you will only continue to lose your life. You will continue to lose the very life, that you never even knew that you had within you.

But, you do have a choice. You can choose your life, or you can continue to choose the process of your death. And if you don't have sense enough to choose life, then I'm choosing life for you! Yes, you are going to save your life today, because to save the life of a Woman is to save the life of a Nation!

The time has finally come, for you to be the Woman of whom you know that you came here to be! The time has finally come, to Restore The Image, The Character, and The Responsibility of this Goddess Blackwoman. And this means "You"! The time has come to spread the wings, that you never even knew that you had.

Dedicated to,
The Blackwoman who is ready to Accept Her Own,
and who has the courage to Be Her Own Self.

The Goddess Blackwoman

Mother of Civilization

Part I

Divine Purpose & Responsibility

"The Mission, The Why, & The How"

The Mother of Civilization
& The Science of Creation

My dear sisters, I pray that almighty God Allah guides these words to your hearts and minds, that they may sincerely inspire you of righteousness. This subject is an important one.

First, in honor to our elders, let me say that this subject is inspired by, and based upon the life-giving teachings of one of the greatest leaders and Master teachers that our Black Nation has ever been blessed to produce; The Honorable Elijah Muhammad. He has proven to be our true brother and our true friend...as well as continues to prove that friendship, more and more everyday, as our understanding develops and matures. We thank almighty God Allah for him, and his message to us. Now, let us enter into this subject matter. "The Mission", "The Why", and "The How.

"To Uplift The Woman, is to Uplift The World"

"To uplift The Woman, is to uplift The World". This is a true fact in deed, to those who understand the Science of Creation. Yet, most of us are ignorant to this science, and neither do we understand the value of the feminine principles of this Universe. As a result, the ignorance of this world has caused and conditioned The

Woman to see no strength, value, nor importance in her own feminine nature.

But, as some of you may already know, The Honorable Elijah Muhammad said to the world that, **"A Nation can rise no higher than it's Woman."** Listen to that. He said that, "A-Nation-can-rise-no-higher-than-it's-Woman." Listen to that carefully. "A Nation can rise no higher than it's Woman."

Now, his teaching to us most definitely indicates that there is an extreme strength, value, and importance to the feminine nature of The Woman. This teaching indicates that the importance of The Woman is so very valuable, that her entire Nation and Society depends upon her and her well being.

But wait now....on the other hand, here we have an entire world today, that sees The Woman and her nature; The Woman and her femininity as worthless, unimportant, purposeless, and unproductive to society. Think about that. Now, whose thinking is it that is actually correct?...this world's thinking, or our brother Elijah's thinking? Who has the proper understanding?

Well, the answer to that question can be found by just taking a close look at this world. Can you imagine a Man of this world fixing his mouth to say that, "a Woman's role is unproductive and unimportant to the building of society", while it was a Woman that produced and built "he himself", plus the entire society of people all around him? Can you imagine that? That is called "arrogant ignorance"...there is nothing worse than a bold stupidity.

Yet, I don't want you to think of yourself as in opposition to a Man, because what is even more tragic, is that Women today themselves have been conditioned to see their own femininity as weak, purposeless, and unimportant to the building of society. And this has caused Women to not even seek out the strengths and powers of their own feminine nature, because the world has taught that the only strength and power to be found, is in the masculine nature, or through the masculine expression. Wrong. This is a misunderstanding.

So, your opposition is not a Man, more than it is a Global Ignorance. This ignorance of misunderstanding and mental-illness has covered the planet so much so, that their are so-called modern-day societies that even sanction the abortion of unborn female children. Sick, sad, sorry, and down right insane this entire world has become, in the ignorance of it's own uncivilized mentality.

It is obvious that this world is extremely lost and needs guidance, instruction, and reprovement. But, who has the strength and authority to correct an entire world that has gone incorrect, other than it's own Mother, The Original Blackwoman? Well? Who is it that will stand up to look this world directly in it's eye, as a "living testimony" that defies the very lie that lurks in the base of it's brain and heart? Well? Who could and should do this other than you...The Mother of All? Who else is there?

"You" are The Mother of every soul on the Planet. The Mother of All that populate The Planet...and as That Mother, it is "your" natural mission to raise your children up into mental maturity....raising the consciousness of your many children around the world, who are suffering under the weight of their own childish foolishness.

Yet, you should know that you can not raise up any consciousness in others, if your own consciousness is not yet raised up. That just can not be done. You can not teach others Self-Love and Self-Respect, if you have yet to love and respect yourself. You can not show others how to be civilized, if you are not yet civilized yourself. Right? Right.

So, what is it that you have to do first? Your first mission is to re-make yourself into the "Living Testimony" that a Blackwoman is in fact The Mother of Civilization; by "thinking civilized" and by "being civilized"...which is merely being yourself! Your True Self!

So, come on and let us delve into this subject matter with some enthusiasm. Let the Re-building and the Reconstruction process begin!

•••••

Okay now, so look...we were discussing how our brother Elijah said to us that, **"A Nation can rise no higher than it's Woman."** That is a serious statement and is the basis of this whole discourse. Yes, that is a very serious statement, but what exactly does that mean? Now, I know that this particular type of teaching sounds good to you, and makes you feel good Blackwoman, but wait a minute. We must look very deeply into those words.

Brother Elijah did not make that statement to just merely inflate your egos or to only make you feel good superficially. No, that was not the purpose. There is much supreme wisdom and supreme science at the root of those words. Listen to the contents of that statement again. **No-Nation-can-rise-higher-than-it's-Woman.** Think about that! Think about what that means! Isn't that something? This means that "your" entire Black Nation can Not Rise in righteousness, until "You" Rise in righteousness yourself, as a Blackwoman.

That is a powerful statement! And it is especially powerful when you begin to studiously dissect the reasons "why" that statement is true. Yet, I repeat that this fact is nothing to boast or gloat in your ego about, but rather this truth indicates a profoundly powerful "responsibility". Yes, this fact indicates the power and importance of "your" Divine Responsibility as a Queen Mother to your many children around this Earth.

The Mother is The First Teacher

See, no "child" can rise higher than the morality and maturity taught to it by it's Mother. Right? Right. How can any "child" be taught, except it has a teacher? And how can it have a teacher except that teacher be it's Mother?

The Mother is every child's very First Teacher! The Mother is every child's most Influential Teacher! She is that child's First Impression! And that First Impression is the Lasting Impression! Do you understand what I'm saying? Of course you do.

Listen, if Mama ain't talking about nothing, the child ain't talking about nothing! If Mama ain't thinking about nothing, the child ain't thinking about nothing! If Mama don't want to do right, the child don't want to do right!

"Children" will imitate their parents, but Mama especially. She is that First Teacher. She is shaping, influencing, and teaching that child even while the child is still in the womb, through the bio-chemistry of her own thoughts! She is most definitely that First Teacher.

You and I have noticed that, even as we grow into adults, we will still sometimes make the same mistakes as our parents did, retain the same habits, and maintain the same character flaws that our parents have, although we should now know much better. But why do we do this? Why is this true about us?

This is true because that "First Impression" is that lasting "form-ative" impression. They call the first beginning years of our lives the "formative years". As children, our First Impressions are consolidated, concretized, and "formed" into the rooted Foundation of which will determine the nature and "form" of everything else in our lives that comes there-after. Read that again.

Just look at your own life today. Everyone of us in here are still being affected by the influential events, occurrences, and exposures that we have experienced during the first six years of our lives...the formative years...the first six days of our creation...or the first six periods of time. These early experiences have "formed" us into that which we are today. Think about it. This is true.

Mother...The Scientist of Creation

Now, after reflecting upon how important and influential your personal relationship and experiences with your own Mother has affected your own personal development, how does this relate to you being "The Mother of Civilization"? Surely there is a parallel to all of this.

If you are the biological as well as spiritual Mother of all Nations and Peoples on this Planet Earth, as a Blackwoman, what purpose of responsibility has this Divine Order of Creation given to you? Well? Have you ever thought about that? Did you know how important you were, and are?...to the well being of your Nation, your Earth, your Universe? Take some time to sincerely reflect about that. We want you to think today.

As a Blackwoman, it is true that "you" have a mission of Responsibility to Uplift "yourself" in Righteousness, Wisdom, Knowledge, Strength, and Pure Spirituality that your entire Black Nation may ascend to do the same! Your well being truly does effect the well being of all. To enrich the soil of your own Fertile Earth, is to enrich everything that grows up out of that Fertile Mother Earth! You are that Mother Earth...a Rich and Fertile foundation of Black Soil...from which all have grown up out of. It is true.

This is exactly why in order to uplift the condition of the whole human family, the condition of the Mother must be uplifted first. It is the simple scientific law of Creation itself. To uplift the whole of Creation, you simply must uplift the components through which it was and is being fashioned...God and his Blackwoman. If she is oppressed, the world oppresses the potentiality of itself. If she is uplifted, the world uplifts the potentiality of itself. Her womb is kin to the substantive darkness of space that bore all of Creation.

You must know to understand these things, and never again let this ignorantly wicked world make you to believe that your life is worthless and purposeless to the building of Civilization. A true civilization can only be built through you. The science of Creation tells you that you are the Cradle and the Cornerstone to any True State of Civilization. Yet you were the cornerstone that the builder's of this world rejected when constructing this ungodly, deteriorating, imbalanced, handicapped, self-defeating, self-destructive so-called state of civilization.

This entire civilization (or lack thereof), has been arrogantly constructed up on one half of the principles of the Universe, while denying the other half. It never could stand on just one leg...and so it has stumbled and fallen unto it's own demise. All of this, because "you" were dis-honored, dis-respected, and rejected...the cornerstone that the builders rejected.

Honor thy Mother that thy days may be long. Dis-honor thy Mother, and your days shall be short lived. You can not honor thy Father alone, and then dis-honor the doorway through which he has come. Curse the Mother and you curse the Father. Honor the Mother and you honor the Father as well. Mother and Father are connected and created of One Divinely Creative Essence.

As a Blackwoman, the more that you grow into the True Knowledge of the True Contents of yourself, the more that you will understand that God Allah has truly blessed you with much...with very much. Powerfully blessed...naturally anointed and appointed, your intuitive nature is godly, when properly cultivated and utilized. But deeply understand that, **"For (she) to whom much is given, much is required."** This indicates Duty and Responsibility as a scientist in the Science of Creation.

Yes, we have learned that, "To Uplift This Woman is To Uplift This World", but whom do you expect to uplift you in "righteousness", uplift you in "wisdom", uplift you in "character", uplift you in "the purpose of responsibility", uplift you in "the value of virtue and morality" other than you? You and Almighty God Allah. And you already know that God will surely help those who are surely helping themselves. Right? Right.

Do you want a "Better" Life? Do you want a "Better" World? Do you want a "Better" You? Well then, You "Better" get up to create what you "want", "will", or "desire" to create. As a woman, you are naturally a co-creator with God. Your "will" of creation operates inside the larger "will" of Creation. God gives you the creative resources by which to create, and you create out of that according to your own "will". So, in whatever state of development you are in, you will naturally create The World around you in your own image and likeness.

"To Uplift The Woman, is To Uplift The World". The Womb of The World. The Womb is fashioned as The Circle. The Circle is The Womb. And The Circle also represents The Circle of People that make up The Society that is produced from that Womb. One Circle comes up out of the inner doorway of another Circle, leaving Circles within Circles. The Mother sits encircled within The Center of The Circles that she has produced.

Raise up the center of a circle, and you will cause the peak of a mountain...in that all that is in the radius of that circle will begin rising up to stand up under the feet of that risen center. The Whole of Civilization will be at her foot...being the firm foundation that lifts her up to be Clothed in the Light of the Sun.

Some of you understand what this means. And eventually we all will. If you do understand this, you understand why "A Nation can rise no higher than it's Woman"...understanding that when you uplift yourself, the world is uplifted, and therefore the world rises to uplift you in return. Divine cause, Divine effect.

You are the scientist of creation. So, rise up...and everything that you produce, shall also be where you are, Blackwoman. Black-Womb-Man. Black Womb of Humanity. Mother of Civilization.

(STOP-THINK)

The Responsibility of
Divine Image & Character

"Ministry of a Thousand Words"

"The Mission, The Why, & The How". We have just learned that as The Mother of Civilization, you have the power to re-make the world into your own image and likeness. But what is your Image and Likeness today? What is your image and character today? If you intend to produce a civilized world, you must become that which you intend to produce.

Now let us cover "some" aspects of the Image and Character of this Goddess Blackwoman...Re-making The Original Impression...The First.

In this particular writing, we want to begin by addressing the subject of Public Image. We want to discuss the issue of your image in the public, as well as it's powerful importance and influence. The image of your character in public is very crucial to the rise of your people at this time, whether you know it or not. This is an important responsibility.

Your Image and Character, in the public, is very important for one basic reason. If you are to accept your own true nature, and your own natural responsibility, as a "Goddess Blackwoman", you are to be a representative of God's peace and God's power to the people.

See, as a "Goddess Blackwoman", you are automatically a representative of God Allah. You are to be the actual container of God Allah's wisdom. You are to be the animated expression of the mind and thinking of Your God. You are a representative of The God who has awakened you from the ignorance of mental death. Really think about that, and dissect the meaning. Do you follow this? This writing is designed to make you think...and this is nothing new, we are just trying to re-kindle your own memory.

A "Goddess Blackwoman", is one in whom The God has poured his character and his wisdom into, and/or has drawn his character and his wisdom up out of. So, if you are to call, label, or seek to present yourself as a "Goddess Blackwoman", you have to be prepared to "real-ize" the true definition of that prestigious and honorable title..."Goddess Blackwoman". Prepare to be yourself.

To "real-ize" the true definition of a "Goddess Blackwoman", you must be willing to persistently strive, or be prepared for the persistent struggle, to bring forth the Highest Qualities of your character, until they become a concrete, rock-solid, permanently projected, constant reality.

Yes, you will become the balance of God's Peace and God's Power. You will project and become a "Peaceful Power" and a "Powerful Peace". That is the balanced character of God.

"Now, wait, wait, wait. Just wait. Hold it. Slow down a minute. What does all of this mean? What is being said here? Break all of this down. What are you talking about? Why should we be so concerned with projecting an external image and character, amidst our people and this World? Why should we even be concerned with how others are viewing us? What is so important about an external image and character? Is this all for selfish vanity?"

These are all very good questions. So, let us investigate these questions, since we know that in order to determine the purity or impurity of an action, we must first determine the purity or impurity of the motivation that prompts the action.

Why be Concerned with Image & Character?

A lot of people sit before the mirror to meticulously primp over their visual image, in order to simply impress others of their external beauty. The motivation is "vain", therefore the action is "vanity". But now think a minute; does this mean that you should totally disregard a meticulous concern for your own image and character? Of course not.

You still may ask, "Well, just why is it so important for a 'Goddess Blackwoman' to be concerned with the refinement of her projected image and character? Why? How can this be important to God and God's Purpose? How can this serve God's Purpose of replenishing the Earth with Righteousness?" Again, this is a very good question, but listen. It is not your mission to merely vainly "impress" people, but rather it is to make an "impression on" the people, as every Mother makes a molded "impression on" the forming character of her child.

Well, if your motive in meticulously refining your image and character is to serve God's Purpose, your actions are divinely inspired. It is your divine mission to teach those of our people who are misguided, the guidance and wisdom that you have been taught. And you teach them through a Word. And your projected image plus the body language of your character speaks Words. And your image is a "Still Picture". And your character is a "Motion Picture". And a "Picture is worth a Thousand Words".

Just the mere "Pictorial" Character and "Visual" Presence of a person illuminated with Divine Intellect, is a Ministry of a Thousand words...a ministry of a thousand words speaking all at once...a picture of the depth of your mind and the condition of your heart, to those that can see it. The Face of God alone can speak Volumes of Wisdom unsaid, and can show Ages of Time unseen...for those that can read its language.

Your Image and Character is a Ministry of a

Thousand Words to all who stand before you. Yet, what is the Message of your Ministry? What are you saying? Everytime that you look at an individual and they look back at you, there is a conversation going on, back and forth. Do you understand? So, what do you have to say, as a "Goddess Blackwoman"? What is it that you are saying, as a representative of God? What needs to be said to this present world? Think about it.

See, this is the reason that our Image and Character is being singled out for study today. It is because that same Image and Character, can, will, and does speak, teach, and minister words unto the people more than our mouths could ever speak at one given time. And, if you are a "Goddess Blackwoman", the words that you speak and teach should be the Words and Principles of Righteousness, Wisdom, or Divine Guidance.

In Submission to God's Duty & Purpose

As any other representative of The God, a "Goddess Blackwoman" is automatically missioned to be a Minister or a Teacher to the people. The God's mission is to teach the Arts & Sciences of Civilization to those who have been deprived of that Knowledge. This will replenish the world with Righteousness. This is The God's Duty and Purpose. And to be in submission to The God's will, is to be in submission to The God's Duty and Purpose.

Well, a "Goddess Blackwoman" is one who has totally submitted to the will of The God, and one who knows what that will is.

A "Goddess Blackwoman" is in submission to The God and The Will of Righteousness. I know that being "in submission" sounds like a passive type of concept, but being "in submission" to "The God" is an **active** or **productive** concept. Oh yes, this is most definitely the truth, because your God is a working, moving, producing, creating, doing, or active being!

Yes, when you truly submit to God, you submit and agree to assist The God at carrying out God's Duty and Purpose. You become an employee or a "worker". Allah is the "employer", and we are the "employees". Of course the wages plus the benefits are excellent! So, we don't complain.

The wages are a Successful Life built on The Principles of Righteousness; and the benefits are the peace of mind and peace with your own soul, that comes from knowing that success. Plus your bonus payment, is the character that you build in the struggle to attain that success. This is true.

In this corporation, you will know that there is surely room to move-up (or spiritually/mentally ascend), for those who will to qualify themselves for that promotion.

This corporation has been assembled to incorporate Righteousness in the Earth. You have been employed to be "a worker" at making this Righteousness a living reality in your everyday life. Your first assignment is to "work" on you...to struggle at incorporating Righteous Guidance in You. Then your second assignment is to share what you have been blessed to find, with all of those who seek to find Righteous Guidance as well. This is what it means to be "in submission to God".

No, this is no passive type of concept. You must persist to "real-ize" the definition of that honorable title, "Goddess Blackwoman". The bottom line point is that, this will involve work and effort.

And don't you worry sister. It is not very hard to be a Righteous Reflection and Representative of The God. All that you have to do is to have the courage to be your Natural Self. Be Yourself. Have the courage. It's okay. How hard can it be to be your own self. They say that it is harder to tell a lie, than to tell the truth. So, it should be harder to "be a lie", than to "be the truth"...which is yourself.

Talk to The World

Let this whole world know that the beauty, strength, and wisdom of our ancient divinity is in deed rising in the West within the hearts and the minds of these forgotten, rejected, and despised former Black slaves. Our mental/spiritual resurrection is now at hand! Let them know.

Of course now, if we are going to let the whole world know this fact, how will we let them know? How? How will you let the entire world know that the righteousness, wisdom, love, and power of Almighty God Allah is again coming to birth within the hearts and minds of these despised former Black slaves? What will be your method? Better yet, how will you let your lost/found brothers and sisters know what is trying to come to birth within themselves? That is the real mission.

And again; how will you do this? Are you just going to "tell" them? Are you going to just tell them with your mouth? Are you just going to sit around pointing out scriptures all day trying to prove to the world that you are the people of God? No, that is not sufficient alone.

Our brother Messenger Elijah Muhammad taught that our beloved brothers and sisters do not need to hear our "lip-service" alone! He instructed that it would be wise to let them know through our "deeds" and "actions"!

We have to show our people (as well as show our own personal selves) through the "deeds" and "actions" of our hearts. Not just "Lip-style", but "Life-style"! That is how you Talk to the World.

Your pattern of "deeds" and "actions" is the foundation upon which your true character is projected. Remember that a visual picture is worth a thousand words. Not just the "still picture" of your outer image, but the "motion picture" of your deeds and actions. So, let your actions and image speak for you. They are going to speak for you anyway, whether you know it or not.

Actions Speak Louder than Words

Humans are motivated by visual stimuli. If your words can't paint the picture, let your actions paint the picture for you. This is better for you. Your deeds and actions are a ministry within themselves. And you had better make sure that you are ministering that which is in accord with Righteous Principle. This is true.

Understand that once you stand-up to be a "Righteous Goddess Blackwoman", in the midst of your down-trodden people, your every action is going to be critically analyzed by all of your brothers and sisters. See, they currently see no benefit in living a righteous life, and "you" serve as "their" personal example. You are their only image of Positivity. You are all that they know of being "into that Black Stuff".

So, if you do something wrong, they are just waiting to critically tear you down, in order to justify living the lifestyle of ignorance and rebelliousness, that their slavemaster has persuaded and conditioned them to presently live. They are awaiting the chance to tear you back down to their level of misery, because this makes them feel more comfortable at living the lifestyle of a fool.

Fools don't feel as foolish, as long as there are a bunch of fools around doing the same foolish things. So, since foolishness plus misery loves company, they will constantly look for a blemish in your character, or an error in your behavior, to cut you back down to the low level that they are living on. And this is what they should do. Yes, they should.

This is just the way it is. You know how our people are, because you are one of them. I know how our people are, because I am one of them. "Negroes" are just like crabs! One always trying to pull back the other! People will search and search and search and search and search for a negative reason to tear you down, when you are trying to get up.

Yes...that's right, so if you fall contrary to the way of

righteousness, they will be there just awaiting the chance to heavily criticize you! And every "Culturally Conscious" Blackman and Blackwoman into that "Black Stuff", that they see striving for a Knowledge of Self, will be judged by your mistake, in the mind of that person. This is the way it is, and this is the way it should be! Oh yes, just think about it.

This is all in the plan. This is God Allah's wisdom. If you claim to be a "Righteous Goddess Blackwoman", and you fall contrary to the way of Righteousness, God Allah will use them negroes to beat-up on your conscience, until you come shamefully running back to the righteous principles that you have abandoned! Do you understand what I'm saying?

I mean, they will dog you out, and look at you with that "I knew them niggas wasn't bout nothin for-real" type of look. I mean, they are just waiting for a reason to kick you when you fall down. But Allah has designed it that way to make sure that we learn to "Stand-up Right" and to "Stand-up Firm". Think about it. Now let us move on.

The Preparation for Duty & Mission

As we have discussed already, to be a "Goddess Blackwoman", is to be a worker or an employee of The God of Righteousness. This means to be a Blackwoman on a Mission, a mission from The God. Your mission is to be a Teacher, Healer, Nurturer, or Saviour of your Nation.

This is nothing new, this has always been the Divine Purpose of The Blackwoman. To be a teacher, healer, nurturer, or saviour is the Purpose of any Mother to her children. You just happen to be The Mother of The World, which gives you a purpose of mission to The World. It is just that the traumatic experiences of oppression have erased the memory of that Divine Purpose from the minds of The Blackwoman.

Now, after this Divine Purpose is brought back to

your memory, how do you prepare yourself for that divine mission to carry out that divine purpose? As we have already discussed, your very first mission as a "Goddess Blackwoman", is to uplift yourself. Your very first mission is to teach, heal, nurture, and save you. That is the focus. You can not uplift anyone else until you are first uplifted. Right?

That is why this is a "Re-Building Effort". What is this? This is a "Re-Building Effort". This is to rebuild that which was destroyed, and to restore that which was taken away. This is to balance that which is imbalanced, and to heal that which is in a state of dis-ease. This is to rebuild and to restore.

So, in order to know what to **rebuild**, we must first investigate to find out what is **destroyed**. In order to know what to **restore**, we must first analyze to find out what is **lost**. In order to **heal**, we must first examine to properly diagnose the places where **dis-ease** exists. And since we are first rebuilding, restoring, and healing ourselves, we must endure a very thorough Self-Examination or personal Self-Analysis.

A Successful Personal Self-Analysis requires the personal strength needed to look harsh-reality directly in the eye. We have to have the courage to be as honest as possible with ourselves. Allright? Be honest to God. This is for your own benefit.

An analysis is an examination, and an examination begins with a series of questions. These questions must be clear, concise, and direct in order to produce answers of the same quality.

To prepare for this thorough upcoming Self-Analysis, start off by addressing some of these initial introductory questions. As with any occupation, job, or mission of work, you must first be Interviewed, Trained, and Qualified to do the work. And a "Goddess Blackwoman" is a worker hired to carryout the mission of The God.

The Interview: "Who are You?"

Now, since you want to be of the Righteous, answer these questions? Allow yourself to be "inner"- "viewed". Come sit down with yourself face to face, and inter-view yourself.

Question: Do "your" thoughts and actions reflect those thoughts and actions of one who is striving for righteousness? Well? Does "your" private and public character reflect the character of the righteous? Well? Who are you?

Do "you" project a righteous image? How well do "you" represent The God? How well are "you" representing yourself as the Queen Mother of the Universe? How well do "you" represent the majesty of the Blackwoman??? Who are you? It's okay, we are just asking a few questions.

Do you know what your duties and functions are on this Earth, as a "Goddess Blackwoman"? Do you know what your purpose is in life, as a "Goddess Blackwoman"?

Well, let us better analyze this thing by looking at a little background information on the task at hand. Let us study the exact Opposite Character of the righteous image that you are striving for. Let us look at the wicked image that this wicked society has taught or conditioned our Blackwomen to become.

The Reality of The Destroyed Blackwoman

As you know, our "Black Queens", and "Black Goddesses" have been mentally grafted by this oppressor. They have had the needle of "self-hate" stuck into their brains, while their original minds were needled out.

This enemy has mentally destroyed and deformed our lost sisters, stage by stage, into a group of (what is now commonly called) "hoes", "bitches", and "thugettes"! Let us just tell the raw truth of the matter here! And the rest of our sisters are either "butt-kissing Aunt-Jemimas", or weak minded "overly submissive Slave Women" who refuse to think beyond the aid of a chauvinistic man that is mentally-ill with the dis-ease of Sexism, because of his own weak insecure self! You know what I'm talking about. Think about it.

That is not the true image of the true Blackwoman! No! No! No! That is not her! That mentally-grafted form is not truly her! That is the way that she was "made", but not "created"! You have to look at this today.

Under the hand of God, The Blackwoman is "created" in the image and likeness of an Intelligently Wise, Morally-Upright, Righteously Civilized, Divine Black Goddess! But, under the hand of this evil white slavemaster, The Blackwoman is "made" into the image and likeness of a rebellious, scrupless, worthless, moraless, scandalous, uncivilized, ignorant, self-hating devil, who manifests in the form of these so-called "bitches", "hoes", and "slavewomen"!!! This is a shame, but this is the truth! Tell that truth the way it needs to be told today! This is real.

And, I'm not just talking about some of these young sisters today, who have been made so Brain Dead, that they will even take pride and seek a reputation as the "badest bitch" or as the most "scandalous ho"! Female musical groups calling themselves "Bitches with Problems" and "Hoes with Attitudes"?

What in this hell is wrong with you? You damn right you got some problems!...More problems than you know. But you are going to solve them Problems and adjust that Attitude today...cause "A Nation Can Rise No Higher Than It's Woman"!!! You are a Woman and you are going to Rise up out of your ignorance or get the hell out of the way! Your Nation is coming up today! Move or be moved!

You know you crazy as hell today, and will produce children that are crazier than you! Yes, I'm talking to "you". Don't start looking around...I'm talking to "you". You just don't know how powerful you are, and that if your mental condition is allowed to stay on that dead level, you can send an Entire Generation of People to death. You are more powerful than you know, and are much more preciously important than you know.

So, ummm...you, ummm, you...you just better get used to acting like yourself again, and not like the damned fool that your slavemaster is trying to make you out to be. Can we talk straight here today? Of course we can, because the condition of your existence will determine the condition of an entire Nation. We can't let these things go on like they have been, can we? We don't want to do that, do we? Don't we want a better life for ourselves and our people? Of course we do, and you better answer like you mean it.

Listen now. And like we have just said, this ain't just talking about some of these younger sisters, but the older Mothers who allowed these misguided young sisters to start acting a damn fool in the first place. Okay? We need some serious straight-talk today.

You always wanting to point the finger of blame at the Youth as if they produced themselves, when you know that the Fruit Don't Fall Too Far From The Tree! Oh now, you know that this is just the truth, so don't be offended. Yes, I'm still talking to "you".

Now listen. How are you going to attempt to divorce yourself from that which you produced from your own womb? If the fruit fell off the tree and rolled over into "utter foolishness", the tree couldn't have been but a few feet from the border of "utter foolishness" itself...if not already across the border. You are the tree! And you trying to act like the fruit fell off the tree and rolled all the way across the apple orchard by itself?

How are you going to blame the fruit for being "bitter", when you know that if the fruit was "sweet", you would be trying to take all the credit for producing such "sweet" fruit. Is that the truth? Yes, you know that's the truth.

Somebody needs to stop all of this perpetrating. We must take responsibility for that which we have produced, by not allowing the same mistakes to be continuously made again. We have got to have the courage to look at the "raw reality" of what this enemy is doing to corrupt "you", therefore our "Mothers", therefore our "Sisters", and therefore our "Daughters"...and therefore our Nation.

Be on guard against this aggression. Be on guard against this oppressor's mentality coming up out of yourself. And, forever be in pursuit of "The Goddess Blackwoman". When you find her, you will have found yourself.

She is Sent From God

But where is that "Goddess Blackwoman" today? Can she be found again? These destroyed, moral-less, mind-less images and caricatures that we see all around, us are the only display of images that our poor Brothers and Sisters know of the Blackwoman today!

They think that this destroyed woman, is the way a Blackwoman is supposed to be! Yet the greatest tragedy is that this Blackwoman also thinks that this is the way she is supposed to be! This is terrible! This is such a grievous thing. But, how could our people know anything different, since this is what they see reflected all around them, everyday? How? How can they know anything different? Well?

How can they know anything different, except that they have an example? And how can they have an example, except she be sent? So, send yourself. Send yourself "Goddess Blackwoman". Send yourself as a Ministry of Righteous Principle! Send yourself as a Messenger of God! Oh, yes. Well, what else did you think that a "Goddess Blackwoman" was to be, during this time, day, and age?

You be you who has sent yourself forth unto yourself, and to your people to shine in the midst of the darkness of ignorance. You be Sent from God. You be drawn up out of the purified waters of Righteousness to extend a cup out to your people thirsting for knowledge of self. You be Sent from God.

"Goddess Blackwoman", you are going to have to project and amplify your Righteous Black image in the midst of our lost sisters, so that our sisters will see "you", and therefore recognize that there is another way! Minister unto your Beloved Sisters! Minister unto your Beloved Brothers! Show them another option of living! Give them a freedom of choice!

Let them know that they do not have to imitate the negative images and stereotypes that the oppressor is projecting for them to be! Give them another image to choose from! Let them imitate you, while you are imitating The God! Can we say that again? Let them imitate you, while you are imitating God!

Let them know that they can now "choose" to stop being the whiteman's "slave-nigga", and start being the righteous Blackmen and Blackwomen that almighty Black God Allah has originally created us all to be!!!

Give your people a choice! You have to hold your clean glass of water up to their dirty glass of water, so that they may be "self-inspired" to clean their own glass of water too! Right? Right? Right!

But wait. Wait now. Wait. Wait, let's calm down here for a minute? Wait. Let us get back to this original point, because in order to be "Sent From The Righteousness of God", you must first "Go To The Righteousness of God".

"Is Your Glass Clean?"

Now, the question is, are we prepared "for the struggle to become prepared" to be "A Ministry of a Thousand Words"? Really, one is in and of itself.

So look, we just discussed that, as a "Goddess Blackwoman", you have to give your people a choice. You are to give them a choice between an upright character or a downtrodden character. And in order to give them that choice, you have to hold your clean glass of water up to their dirty glass of water, that they may be "self-inspired" to clean their own glass of water as well.

But the question now is, "Is your glass clean?" Is-your-glass-clean? Is your glass clean? Yes, we have to talk about this. Come on and tell the truth. We can talk candidly with one another. This is just between me and you, I'm not going to tell anybody. Relax, reflect, and go ahead and answer this question honestly. This is still part of "The Inter-view".

Is-your-glass-clean? Is it as clean as it is could be? Does your glass of water even appear to be clean? How does it look? Go ahead and look at it. Self-reflect for a second. Inter-view yourself.

Now, you know that if your glass of water looks just like those same persons of whom we are supposed to help, then I guess that we are in pretty bad shape. That is no good. I'm sure you understand that we can not stimulate any righteousness in someone else, if we are not righteously stimulated ourselves. Now, can we? You can't give what you ain't got. We can't stress that point enough.

So, the question is asked again. Is your glass of water clean? How often do you clean it? Does it stay clean at all times? These are the types of questions that we need to ask ourselves on a continual basis, to insure our continual steady growth.

The Interview (cont.)

Here, let's talk a little more about this thing. We are just asking questions for the sake of self-development. So, just be totally honest. Okay? Okay.

We want to constantly ask ourselves questions and re-view our behavior. We are constantly seeking the reprovement of ourselves. There is always room for improvement in a person who has a Divine Infinite Potential. So, we always keep a watchful eye on The Self. And we Question The Self.

We will turn to The Self, and constantly ask questions like these. "When you are in the company of your old friends, does your renewed righteous image remain pure? Or do you fall back into your former Image and Character of Ignorance?"

Do you allow your glass to be dirty, for a minute, so that you can be considered "one of the girls" again? Or do you remain in tact, pure and strong, so that your old girl-friends may be motivated to stop being "one of the girls", and grow-up to be "One of the Righteous Blackwomen" that they are supposed to be? Huh? Well?

Okay, so now just who are you exactly? Who are you today? Is your Image and Character a projection or reflection of The God, just as the moon reflects the light of the Sun, or even as the Sun boldly projects it's essence from it's own core? What do you reflect from your surface or project form the core of your own being? Who are you today?

Do you consider yourself to be a "Righteous Goddess Blackwoman", but yet you are still projecting the same old Image and Character that you used to, back in the days of ignorance? Are you? You can be honest with yourself. Are you really who you say you are? Do you really want to become who you say you want to become? Why are you here?

Look, let me ask you a question. Is it that, deep-down inside you are really still just the same old mentally-dead, no-good, evil-acting, negro that you have always been, but now you just have a Righteous Front? Uh-oh. Are you Perpetrating a Fraud? Are you a Symbol with no Substance? Is this you? Uh-ohhh. Be honest, now.

Well, this type of behavior can't be continued. You can't go on like that. No, the reason that we have come here to this conversation in the first place, is to stop living a lie.

Don't think that you are just going to drop one lie, and pick-up another. No, that just will not help you today.

You can only walk with One Master. You first have to deny yourself. You have to deny your old self, in order to meet with your new self, which is your true self. And if this previously described behavior describes you, it's okay; because whatever is wrong with us today, we are going to fix it with the help of almighty God-Allah. Is that right? I said, is that right? Of course, that is right...you better start answering like you mean it.

You can answer all of these questions by meticulously, studiously, relentlessly, and firmly examining your own personal thoughts and your own personal actions. Look at yourself. Don't be afraid, just look. You can tell a tree by the fruit it bares.

So, objectively step outside of yourself and look at your projected Image and Character. What is the condition of the fruit that you are currently reaping? Sweet or Sour? Stand before the mirror of your conscience.

Are you still manifesting the same characteristics of yesterday? Take a good long "honest" look at yourself Goddess Blackwoman of Righteousness. It's okay. This is just between you and your heart. And Allah is knower of what we hide and what we manifest. So, just tell the truth.

Listen beloved Blackwoman. You are particularly required to undergo a very thorough purification process. You are so very important. You are so very valuable. You are so very precious. I still don't think that you understand that yet.

You are to give birth and rise to a Nation of Divine Gods and Goddesses. You are a "Virgin Mother" giving birth to Saviours. The word "virgin" only signifies "purity". One who is "Pure", gives birth to "Purity".

You will become purified as you intercourse with the Wisdom of Divine. And then The Pure Spirit (or The Pure Mind of God) shall come upon you and become in you. Thereafter, everything that you touch, build, do, and give birth to, will be absolutely Divine, hereafter. That is why it is said that Heavenly Paradise lies at the foot of The Woman. Sister, you are that Woman. If only you understood, how real your God is.

Understand that, in order for you to nurture and nurse this world back into a healthy state of righteousness, your Mother's Milk of wisdom must be totally purified into its healthiest state for it to have the Potency to restore the mental health of your Nation (your children). Purified Milk can only be produced from a Purified Mother.

Again, our brother Messenger Elijah Muhammad taught us, **"A Nation Can Rise No Higher Than It's Woman."** Think over that. This indicates "The Mission", "The Why", and "The How". Your Divine Purpose and Your Divine Responsibility.

"Let Us Make Woman"
(The Self-Analysis)

Allright now, are you ready? "Ready for what?" Are you ready to 'Let Us Make Woman'? "How do you want to Make Her?" Let Us Make this Woman in the image and likeness of Divine. "Why?" Because, she is already Divine. We just have to make her to know what she truly is, so that she can be what she truly is. Allright? "Allright then." Well, 'Be and it is'. Be and it is.

Let Us Make Woman. Let You Make You. Let You Make A New Woman. Let you Re-create Yourself all over again in the Image and Likeness of a "Goddess Blackwoman".

You are now like unto a genetic-engineering scientist, in that you are a "Character-Engineering Scientist". You go into the seed, core, and coding of your own heart to cut out character traits that are not of God or Righteousness, and you place in those that are. You are Re-Creating The Character of your Being. Let Us Make Woman. Let Us Make Woman. Let Us Make "Goddess Blackwoman".

Proceed with the Purification Process. As stated before, we want to look into the mirror of our Own Conscience. We want to see our own "Self-Reflection", or we want to use our minds to "Reflect about Self".

And in order for you to sincerely analyze and evaluate The Self, you must mentally step outside of your own personal Point of View. Okay? To do this, just simply visualize yourself from someone else's perspective, walking up to you to meet you for the first time. Go ahead. Visualize this in action. Take an honest look at "you", and assess what it is that you see. Who are You?

What do you see? Do you like what you see? Take a look. Look at her. Walk up to her. Talk to this person for a while. Do you see, reflected in this person, the same qualities that you respect in other people? Who are You? Visualize this thing.

After interacting with this person, do you admire the qualities and characteristics that you see in this person (which is you)? After looking and talking to "you" from the perspective of another person, what do "you" think about "you"? **Are "you" the type of person that "you" would respect, admire, and seek as a friend?** Answer that question.

That is an extremely important question! So, please read that again and again and again, because **the only way that "you" can truly love and respect "you" is to <u>be</u> what you truly love and respect.**

Go ahead, read that again, and again, and again...and then go write that down on something where you may see it and read it everyday. Go ahead. For real...Go write it down. We can continue as soon as you return.

Wait...as a matter a fact, I'll write it down for you. Here, just take this next whole page and photocopy it. Tack this paper on to your mirror, your refrigerator, your wall, your door, or someplace where you will see it everyday. But you go and write it down yourself, until you get the chance to photocopy it. This will be our Affirmation for Life.

The only way that "you" can truly love and respect "you", is to "be" what you truly love and respect.

The Affirmation for Life
Goddess Blackwoman

Gaining a Knowledge of Self through "Self-Talk"

Now look, we are all on a quest for a Knowledge of Self. But, that does not just mean the history of our people, that also means a knowledge of the personal history of yourself, which reveals the real contents of yourself to yourself...a Knowledge of Self.

So, let's look at who you are right now today, that you may determine who you want to be, and who you will become tomorrow, with the help of God Allah.

To know The Self, one must Look at The Self. Self-Reflection...to Contemplate about Self. Self-Reflection begins with "Questioning Self" (or to Quest-into Self). Communicate with Self. Converse with Self. Sit down and have a discussion with Self. You will not be insane if you do this, but you may stay insane if you don't.

They say that every healthy relationship is based on "good communication". So, how else can you establish a healthy relationship with your own self if you don't sit down and have a good talk with your own self every once in a while? No, I ain't crazy, you just listen.

I said, how else can you establish a healthy relationship with your own self if you don't sit down and have a good talk with your own self every once in a while? You have been living with you for all of these years, and you don't even know your own self. You act like strangers. You don't even speak to one another. You have no real relationship with one another. You don't even like to look at one another. You always trying to get away from around one another. You always trying to get away from the reality of "you". This is because you don't like "you". And this is because you have no Knowledge of Self.

You can't learn to like somebody that you refuse to even sit down and talk to. You never know, you might like you after all, once you get to know you.

So, start getting acquainted. Don't be ashamed. Talk to you. Get to know you. Ask yourself some questions.

See if you are even worthy to have a relationship with you. Do you like who you are? Are you attracted to what you are? How can you become that which is attractive and respectable to your own self?

Sit down and have a little conference with you. Get things straight between you. Cross-examine yourself. See if you are altogether who and what you say you are. See if you are altogether who and what you say you want to be. Do you solemnly swear to tell the truth and nothing but the truth? So, help you God.

Look in the mirror of your conscience and cross-examine yourself and your behavior. Ask yourself a few questions of Self-character. Find out who you are. This is still The Inter-view or The Inner-view. We want to know Self. We want to know the Good and the Bad of our Character.

We intend to Clean-Up The Bad, and Enhance The Good through this next Self-Reflection process called "Character-Cleansing". It is only an introductory character-cleansing, but it will be a cleansing. It will be a process. We do intend to open up the heart of your character, and the brains of your thinking. How else can a doctor operate? And you are that doctor.

You are the scientist of Character Cleansing Surgery, and all of your character illnesses must be made manifest to you before you know what to cleanse. Can you handle this type of open-heart surgery? Can you? This is what it takes to reprove and steadily improve yourself. This is what it takes to restore "The Goddess Blackwoman". So, let the surgery begin.

• • • • •

Question: Who are you?

Answer: I am a Blackwoman on a Mission.

Question: And what Mission is it that you are on?

Answer: I am on a Mission to fulfill the duties and purposes of a "Goddess Blackwoman", which is my True Self.

Question: What are the Duties and Purposes of a Goddess Blackwoman?

Answer: My Duties and Purposes are to Restore and Replenish the qualities of Righteousness into my own self first, and then to the masses of my downtrodden people.

Question: Do you have The Righteous Image and Enduring Character to support and carry out such a taskfilled responsibility?

Answer: I strive and struggle to reprove and improve the Purity of My Image, the Strength of My Character, and the Understanding of My Responsibility on a constant daily basis.

Question: Are you ready to discuss the first phases of "Character Cleansing" as put forth in the second part of this writing?

Answer: I am. Let us grow on.

Part II

Divine Image & Character

"12-Points of Character Cleansing"

(Do we still do the things that we used to?)

Character Reflection #1

"Attitude/Character Projection"

Do we still do the things that we used to? Do we still have the same projected Attitude and Character, as we did before we had any Knowledge of Self? Who are we today? What is your projected Attitude and Character? Let's look at it.

How is your projected attitude when you come in contact with other people? Are you as **courteous** as possible to people, or do you have an image of **rudeness**? Is your aura **positive**, or is it **negative**? Do you **inspire** people, or do you **depress** them? Who are you?

Do you **smile**, or do you **frown**? Do you project **peace**, or do you project **chaos**? Are you **warm**, or are you **cold**? Do people feel very **attracted** to you, or do they feel **repulsed** or **rejected**? Who are you today?

When people come into contact with you, do they feel renewed, revitalized, and refreshed by your quickened, and spiritually positive attitude or vibrations? Or are they just left to feel nothing from you, because your Attitude and Vibrations match that of the average mentally dead negro? Who are you today? Where is the beauty of that "Goddess Blackwoman"?

Do you give people a feeling of **hope**, or do you

further influence their feelings of **despair**? Does your attitude still suggest that "niggas ain't nothin", and are headed for destruction and doom? Or does your attitude suggest that salvation for the Blackman and Blackwoman is now at hand!? Well? Look at it now. We all must answer these questions. We all must take this thorough look at the Self.

Well, if any of this negative behavior describes you, what could be the deeper lying roots to this type of death projecting behavior? Is it that you are just "afraid" to outwardly Express Love? Or do you even have any Love in Your Heart to express? Hmmm? Do you **love** your people, or do you still **hate** them? Do you hate yourself? Are you mad at God about something?

What is the root of this behavior? Just what are the True Contents of your Heart? What is at the Base of Your Brain? Why are You Here? What is Your Motivation. Why is Your Character this way? Why is Your Heart so Desolate of Love, but so full of Hate for Self, and therefore everyone else? Let's talk about this today. We are just asking questions. Think about it a while.

This type of questioning should not bother a person who is looking for improvement and reprovement. Right? So, it shouldn't bother you, if you are here for the reason that you say you are here. Right? A person who is genuinely looking for higher development, will gladly search for their imperfections, that they may perfect them! Isn't that what you are here for?

So, just willfully and honestly look to see which of these attributes, positive or negative, that you are manifesting. Determine which of these manifested attributes are of God Allah, and which are not, so that you will know which manifested character attributes to keep and which to discard away. Simple. You don't have to get your little feelings in the way. Isn't that what you are here for?

This process is called "Character Cleansing".

Right? This is the true "Brain-washing". Right? We are going to wash The Brain and The Heart of all impurities that impede us from rising into The Success of our own Innate Divine Potential! Is that right? Is that right? Now, can I get an "Amen"? Amen (let it be).

Don't you want to fulfill your own Potential? Don't you want The Success of Life? Well, alright then...adjust your positive attitude according to the positive purpose for which you have come. Now, we can and will positively proceed. Come on.

"Act"ualize God

Now listen. What have we come here to do? What have we entered into this discussion for? The title of this book says that we are here to "Re-store The Image, The Character, and The Responsibility, of The Goddess Blackwoman". We need to be clear. We need to be clear.

I don't think that we are quite clear on what this whole "Goddess Blackwoman" thing is all about. We don't quite understand what that title and term means. We need to be clear about this. Now, what is a "Goddess Blackwoman"? I want you to dissect that term or title apart today. Get clear on this.

"Goddess Blackwoman". Split that whole title apart into it's halves and quarters, in order to clearly grasp who and what you are supposed to be. Look at that term in it's granulated particle form. "God-dess-Black-Wo-man". That is an equation.

If you know how to add these particles together, you will come up with an interesting summation. You will begin to deeply understand that The God should be alive and well, living, growing, and glowing within you! This is very important.

You will understand that you are supposed to be the temple and the womb of "THE LIVING GOD"! The God Essence should be within the triple dark Black Infinity of your Womb/Mind. Allah should be in the person of you! Do you understand what that means? Do you? Are you sure? No you don't. You don't know what that really means, so listen...come on, just listen.

Here, for right now, let us just look at it from the perspective of our given subject matter of "Attitude & Character Projection".

If we take into consideration all that has been said, who's Attitude and Character are you to project, as a "Goddess Blackwoman"? Who is The Paradigm, The Measure, and The Example by which you are to pattern and adjust your own Attitude and Character? Obviously, your God is The Paradigm and The Measure. You are to project the Attitude and Character of The God.

"Yes, I know this. But what exactly does that mean?" "What is the Attitude and Character of The God?" "And how can I project this? What does this actually mean?"

In "act"-uality this means that God Allah should be living, breathing, thinking, acting, hearing, seeing, speaking, and manifesting through you! Through who??? Through you! Who else? This is what it "act"-ually means.

Your enemies are called "the synagogue of satan" all throughout the scripture, but you are called "THE TEMPLE OF THE LIVING GOD". You are the throne of Allah.

Yes, this is you. I am still talking directly to you...right there, so make no mistake. You are more than what you think yourself to be. "You are the throne of Allah". The God should be sitting atop of your brains governing, managing, orchestrating, and animating all of your affairs and actions. Do you understand what I'm saying? God should "act"-ually be manifested in the person of you.

The Image and Character of The God should come right across The Wisdom of your Thoughts, The Purity of your Heart, The Screen of your Face, The Tone of your Voice, and The Spirit of your Personality. This is Our

Goal...to "act"-ualize The Peace, Power and Principles of The God of Righteousness in our Person. Can you handle that? Do you understand? Sure you do. The Goal is only to be yourself again. Think about it beloved Blackwoman.

A Goddess Blackwoman is a Woman in whom The God is alive and vibrant. This means that if a drug-dealer meets you, he should feel like he just met God in the person, and an overwhelming internal feeling of shame should cloud his mind. His conscience should start talking to him, because the strength of the God in you has stimulated the voice of the God within his own mind. That drug-dealer shouldn't even be able to look you in the eye, unless he or she is ready to repent, reform, and respect themselves.

But wait now. Please do not take this out of the proper context. Wait. Slow down. Don't get carried away. Wait. Yes, I'm still talking to you.

For This Reason, I was Born into The World

All of this does not mean that you will stand there and "self-righteously" scold, condemn, or put-down any of your brothers or sisters. No. This will be no excuse for you to continue being hateful towards your own people. No. This is about the Love of Self and the Love of your Own Kind. We all have our own personal trials and weaknesses to overcome. Remembering that fact, will naturally give you a patient compassion with your own people. So, remember.

An egotistical "self-righteous" posture is incorrect, especially when you know that you are just "five minutes out of foolishness" yourself...and so am I. Now, isn't that right? Our duty is not to dis-respect or dis-regard our downtrodden people. Our duty is to heal these wounds.

A doctor or "healer" does not arrogantly shun his patients because they are sick. That would not make much sense, now would it? No. The healer looks at the ill-patient and says, "...for this reason, I was born into The World." That is the right attitude. Think over that. That is the Attitude and Character of God.

The bottom line lesson here only means that you should always be striving to have your own self together to such a high and righteous, moral degree, that you will not even have to say a word.

Your strong, plus sincere, image and character will say it for you. Remember that a picture is worth a thousand words. The projection of a righteously divine Attitude and Character will speak volumes for you, wherever you go.

The prostitute should not even be able to see you without automatically reflecting on the condition of her lifestyle. The crack-addict should see your righteous Black image in their conscience, everytime that they even just think of lighting-up that pipe! The thief should drop their head in shame, everytime you are in their presence!

Also, any type of aggressive evil should feel highly uncomfortable around you! The devil should either be trying to kiss your feet, or scurry away from around you! You should fear no evil! Evil should fear the light of The God coming from you! Two opposing opposites can not occupy the same space at the same time. One has to give way to the other. Now, who is going to give way?

The **ignorant** should desire **to know**, after meeting you. The **foolish** should be inspired to seek **wisdom**, after meeting you. The **hopeless** should have **hope** after meeting with The God in you. And the **insecure** should rest in the **security** of an assured mind after meeting you. They'll know everything is gonna be allright. Yes...for this reason, "you" were born into the world.

The Atmosphere of God

Your properly projected Divine Attitude and Character can inspire and stimulate all of these things in other people as well as your own self. A divine Attitude and character can produce profound effects.

Question: How does Attitude and Character do all of these things?

Answer: To know exactly how Attitude and Character has such a profound effect, you must know exactly what an Attitude and Character is.

Question: Exactly what is an Attitude and Character?

Answer: A positive or negative Attitude is a particular rhythm, or pattern of positive or negative "thought", turning over and over in your brain. This internal revolving pattern of thought produces and projects your character outward. Your outward character is simply the rhythm and pattern of your thoughts, projected through your speech and actions (verbal and bodily language).

The rhythmical pattern of thoughts revolving in your brain "act"-ually produces an electrical charge that overtakes your atmosphere (or atoms in your spherical domain). At any given time, you can and are doing this.

You carry your Atmosphere with you wherever you go. Your attitude is emitted outward and encases itself around you and anybody else who is within your atmosphere. This is why, when you go around some people, they can pull your spirit down or they can lift your spirit up. Or sometimes you will feel a good vibe or a bad vibe.

Vibe, is short for vibration. Your Attitude will determine the rate of frequency by which these "act"-ual atoms in your atmosphere will vibrate. And whosoever has the attitude that is most dominate in the Atmosphere, will control the dominant vibe, mood, tone, or feeling of the atmosphere.

We say all of this to make you very, very, very clear of how powerful your Attitude and Character Projection is. We don't want you to make any mistake on how important all of this is. None of these teachings are for any vain reasoning. This is real. This is science . This is real.

Your projected Attitude and Character is the

substance of your Atmosphere. Since, you carry your Atmosphere with you, you can "act"-tually effect all that is around you, and not even be aware of it. Being a "Goddess Blackwoman", means that you carry The Atmosphere of God with you.

When you project and place this Atmosphere on, in, and around people, you can heal or help them, as well as yourself, in ways that you have yet to be conscious of. This is nothing spaced-out or crazy. This is just science. And so are you. You are just science. An Atmosphere is a Sphere of Atoms. A Sphere of Atoms are the "act"-ual moving material particles of which you are made up of. God is Real.

Final Affirmation:

A"God-Essence-Blackwoman" projects the Peace, Power, and Presence of Divinity in Person.

Carry The Atmosphere of God wherever you go, and it will carry you also."

Character Reflection #2

"Maturity"

So now that we know what your character <u>should</u> project, what <u>does</u> your character project? Are you projecting the character of the "Righteous Goddess Blackwoman"? Let us see into this. Let us see into Self.

Let's talk about "maturity". Do we still do the things that we used to? Do you still act silly, like an immature little girl? What is your character? Come on, we can talk. Do you act goofy and dilly like most non-thinking caucasian women? Are you light-headed and giggly all of the time as if you have not a serious thought in your mind? Is this your character? Tell me something. What is so amusing? What is so amusing about the condition of our people today? This "death" is not amusing.

Do you constantly act silly as an attempt to escape and run from the serious realities of your life, or from the silent voices of your conscience? Think about it. We do this a lot. Do you joke around entirely too much? Is this your character?

Is this how you imagine the character of God to be as well? Is this the character that you see when you think of a strong, upright, wise Goddess Blackwoman? Well, is it? What do you see? I'm asking you. What do "you" see, when you think of a strong, upright, wise Goddess Blackwoman?

Invision in your own mind the image and character of any Wise and Responsible person that you know of, and that you respect. Think of the historical ones as well as the ones you may know of today that you respect. Think of all the Wise Sages. Think of all the Wise Master Teachers. Invision them. Think about them. Does your vision show them to be acting a fool all of the time? You tell me? Well? How do you see their character? What is their dominant behavior?

If you respect this person or persons that you have invisioned, what qualities do you see in them, that you respect so much about them? Well? And, if you want to become respectable to your own self, shouldn't you attempt to reproduce those same qualities within your own character towards the enhancement of your own individual personality? I would think so. You should think so too.

But notice one thing. You do not invision these individuals, of whom you respect, to be "constantly" laughing, joking, playing, and acting the fool all of the time. You see them as The Wise. You see them as a Mature Self-Controlled Individual. When you look into their eyes, you see a Focused Depth of Thought. This is why you respect them.

And it is these same Ones of whom you respect, that make great accomplishments in the history of their lives and ours. These Great Ones, of whom you respect, don't take their lives for a joke...nor do they naively take it for granted. They take their lives very seriously. And they make serious accomplishments and contributions to life for us all. That is why their names are honored and respected by us, long after they have passed away. They took their life seriously and did something constructive with it.

The Priority of Work & Play

Listen, this life that we live is not simply for sport, fun, party and play. No, this life is not a trivial thing. And you don't live this life in a trivial pursuit. No, this life is not a vacation trip for your personal mindless entertainment. No, this would be a blatant disrespect to your Creator.

Why would your God take his Personal Time and Mind, to Masterfully and Meticulously weave together each Individual Microscopic Sub-Atomic Particle of Matter, that is functioning to make up **"your"** Specifically Engineered Anatomical Design, unto a Living, Breathing, and Thinking Creation, just for you to giggle your life away in sport and play with that thoughtless vacant look in your eyes? Don't insult your Creator like that! Don't waste your Creator's time and mind. Don't insult your Creator like that. You would be insulted too...and rightfully so.

The Maturity of our Minds has never seemed to catch up with the physically developed Maturity of our bodies. Our mental growth has stagnated in the aging process, while our bodies age on. We are now just "older children" that can't run as fast and jump as high as the "younger children". We are the children with arthritis and back pain, but children all the same. All of us together, playing our lives away in trivial pursuit. Look at that.

We still think as a child would think. We still see the world through the eyes of a child. We still want everything "our way" all of the time, even though we have supposedly grown up into adult life. But "our way" is still too childish. Having things "our way" would be fine, if "our way" of thinking was more mature. But, our thinking is still too small, too petty, too selfish, too spoiled, and too immature. We are adults that still want to play games all day and night. Yet, when you get older, you learn that this life already has it's Own Way and Own Order. This Universe has a priority to it's order.

This-Life-Has-A-Priority-To-It's-Order. Right? The Sun works to shine all the day long before it sets to rest. This tells us that Play and Rest come after the priority of Work is done. This tells us that Laughter and Amusement come after the priority of the Serious Issues are first resolved and dealt with. This is because, if you don't take care of business first, you will not have too much to be amused nor entertained about later.

It is your oppressive adversaries, that are consistently striving to keep you so full of amusement, and so full of entertainment, that they may keep you diverted from the real issues and goals of your life.

The longer that they can keep you amused, entertained, and diverted from reality, the more that they can continue to rob you of the real riches of livelihood. They are feverishly in pursuit of "their life", liberty, and happiness...as well as in pursuit of "yours" too! They have their own livelihood plus all of yours too!...and living happily ever after.

But you are satisfied with the entertaining amusement that they feed you 24 hours a day. And at the end of that day, you are left with a silly grin on your face and a vacant stare in your eye, while they are left with this Whole World in the palm of their hands. Now you ask yourself, what's so amusingly funny about that? Nothing. Nothing at all.

Listen. We all want to enjoy life. We all have a sense of humor. We all "need" a little playtime. We all "need" to be entertained here and there. Yes, we all "need" these things.

But the question is, "Do **'you need'** a little playtime right now, if you have already been playing for half of your precious life"?

The question is, "Do **'you need'** to be entertained right now, if you have already entertained away half of your precious life?"

What do **"you need"**? Do you even know what **"you"**

"<u>need</u>"? Do **"<u>you need</u>"** to be Educated, or Entertained? Just look at the present condition of **"<u>your life</u>"**, and reflect on the question again. Is **"<u>your life</u>"** all that it would, could, and should be? Hmmm? Well, there is your answer. Maybe it's time to get more serious about your life.

To all things, there is a season. There is a season for work, and there is a season for play. There is a proper season, place, situation, and priority for all things. Now, what season is it today?

Everybody needs balance in their lives. An **"overworked"** person **"<u>needs</u>"** playtime in their life for balanced-stability, sanity, and health. But an **"over-played"** person **"<u>needs</u>"** productive worktime in their life for balanced-stability, sanity, and health. Now, looking at the condition of our people, what do **"<u>we need</u>"** for balanced-stability, sanity, and health?

They say that "laughter is good for the soul". But don't you forget that "thinking is good for your Brains". And if your brains are deprived of the light and life of serious intelligent thought, pretty soon your soul will be deprived of it's light and life too. Remember that. "You" had better know what **"<u>you need</u>" to balance, stabilize, and create a successful life "for you".**

Raising The Child in Us & The Need for Supervision

It is our "needs" that must be fulfilled, not necessarily our "wants"...unless we are wise enough to "want" what we "need". And the "need" of our people today is "proper guidance", as is the need of any child, or immature person. The "need" of a child can only be fulfilled by an adult who is maturely wise enough to recognize the "need" of that child, and fulfill that "need". We have been mental and spiritual children. The "need" of the child is "proper guidance".

This means that a Goddess Blackwoman can only be

an effective Mother to her Civilization, by having the Maturity of Proper Guidance ingrained within her. She must be "properly guided", before she can "properly guide". And this is the purpose for which we are reading at this very moment. Don't forget that we are rebuilding and preparing ourselves for a responsibility. We must be prepared.

The way that you practice and prepare for the responsibility of raising children, is by first raising up the immaturity of yourself...or raising up the child within self. This only means to wisely and maturely guide, nurture, and discipline the childish aspects of your own character unto the maturity of it's potential.

You already have the substance and principles of Maturity in you, it is just that they are not being fully empowered and expressed. It is that childishness, in most of us, that is running the show. The "child in us" is running our lives.

But you and I know that if a child is left to run the house and follow it's own will, it will play and eat candy all day long until it makes it's own self sick. Right? Pretty soon, if that child is left unchecked and undisciplined, the child will play itself unto it's own demise. A child may drink some poison, or set the house on fire just for the sheer entertainment of watching the flames! This is why there must be adult supervision. Yes, an adult super-vision is what is needed.

Super-Vision is just another word for Wisdom, or the ability to see what most other's can not see. This Vision of Maturity is gained from the study of one's own Time of experiences, and/or seeing that of others.

You already have this Maturity of Wisdom in you. Just give that Maturity the authority to Supervise you. You already have this Good Sense. Just give that "Good-Sense" the power over your thoughts and actions. "Good-Sense" is really "God-Sense". "God-Sense" is really "Super-Vision". And this you were born with.

You already know right from wrong. Right? Right. You have always known right from wrong, but yet always have found it difficult to do what you know, you know, you "need" to do. There is that word "need" again.

Well, this is all rooted in a lack of Mature Supervision, because a child can not fulfill it's own "needs". And, in our lives today, it is the child that is running the adult. The tail is running the head. But, a tail can't see where it's going because it has no guiding super-vision. The head has eyes for super-vision, but yet it is facing in the wrong direction traveling backwards. This is the classic case of the Blind leading the Blind. This we must change. The head must take charge. The adult must command authority within us.

Your Child Is Watching You

We all know that we are not doing what we could, should, and would do. And this verifies that there is some Principle of Mature Guidance present in us, because we do recognize that we are not being as properly guided as we wish. We can see this. And seeing this fact hurts us, and leaves us feeling dissatisfied. Seeing that we are not living up to our potential, really hurts us deeply down inside. Seeing this reality about ourselves, will subconsciously destroy our character, whether we consciously acknowledge this reality as truth or not. Seeing this, slowly erodes our self-esteem bit by bit. Seeing this, robs us of our own self-respect. Seeing this, depletes us of our own self-love. And this is not so good.

Now, this is really why your Image and Character is so very important. We can not stress this enough. Your Image and Character is not only what is seen on the outside, but what is "In-visioned".

Listen, this rebuilding process is not to show others your greatness, but it is to show your own self, your own greatness! This is not to vainly make others believe in you, but to make you a true believer in yourself!!!! Can you hear this Blackwoman!?!?! This is about You! and You! and You!

This power of belief in the "Good-ness" in You, will erupt the awakening of the "God-ness" in You, and only then...for unto us a Goddess is Born! A Sun-Light is given! And A Nation Shall Be Upon Her Shoulders! And she shall be called Wonderful! Counselor! A Mighty Goddess! The Everlasting Queen Mother! The Princess of Peace! Yes, yes, yes, yes, "you"!!!

This is real and none of these words are idle words. There is a purpose behind them all. This is no vain nor trivial pursuit either. Now, let us calm down and continue with this subject...for we have not yet ascended unto our ultimate destinies. Where were we? Oh yes, here we are.

We were discussing how, the true importance of our Image and Character, is to monitor how we personally invision, and discern the level of Maturity within ourselves. We were discussing the importance of How We See our own selves...our own Self-Opinion...Self-Opinion.

See, they say that it is important to be careful of how you act around children, because they see, hear, and pick up on everything that you do. Well, since, in most cases, we are the biggest child that we know, we need to be very careful about how we act around our ownselves! The only child that is most carefully watching you, is "the child within you". Who? "The child within you"...that part of your character that wants to be undisciplined and immature. "The Child within You".

What principles are you showing and teaching this child? This is the question we must ask. You are this child, and you are also the adult. Can this child respect the adult in you? Is the adult in you even alive or presently expressed as an example to the child? If so, what admirable principles are you showing this child, that would gain it's respect for you (which is actually self-respect)?

Of course this child will not respect you, nor seek your guidance, if it sees you behaving as immaturely as itself, if not more immaturely, than it's own self. Right? This is true. A child is not as foolish as you may think. A fool, who will not follow another fool, must now be considered "wise".

So, since this "child in you" is watching you, can this child look up to you? Or can this child only see you on the same level eye to eye, because your behavior is just as immature as any other child?

Your pattern of behavior should always be an example of "proper guidance" to your child. "You" are always watching "you". And what you do will always have an effect on your own respect for self, and your self-esteem. So, always strive to be that which you yourself could and would respectfully look up to. Be a good example for yourself. Does that make sense? Sure it does.

Spend Your Good-Sense Maturely

You already have "Good Sense". And you already know how to use and spend your "Good Sense" maturely. Yes, you do. Just begin to do it. Just begin to use it. Start right now.

Question: If you have the choice to fill your brains with 5 hours of Enriching Education, as opposed to the 5 hours of Amusing Entertainment, that your adversary is trying to feed you, which one of these "investments of time" would give you a full profitable return on your "investment of time"? Think about it. You are the mathematician, add it up. See, I told you that you naturally had good-sense, we just have to start choosing to utilize it, to our own advantage.

You already had sense enough to know what would be the best "investment of your time". Your life itself is an "investment resource". All that your life consists of, is a reservoir, an embankment, an account, or an amount of time, that is available to you. It is available to you to "spend it wisely" or "blow it foolishly". Spend it to your benefit and spend it Maturely. Do not spend it immaturely in trivial pursuit. Invest productive and constructive activities into "Your-Life-Time", to see a constructive and productive profit in, and from "Your-Life-Time". Enrich your mind first, and all other things shall be added unto you in their proper priority. That is the Mature thing to do. We will talk more about "time" later.

Question: What is the equation for Maturity?

Answer: Wisdom + Discipline = Maturity. 4 degrees of Wisdom + 4 degrees of Discipline = 4 degrees of Maturity, 6 degrees of Wisdom + 6 degrees of Discipline = 6 degrees of Maturity and so on and so forth. Infinite Wisdom + Perfect Discipline = Supreme God. We are the children of that Supreme God. God serves as Our Nurturing Mother. God serves as Our Guiding Father. "Nurture" with the maturity of "Wisdom". "Guide" with the maturity of "Discipline". All of us children must Mature in Time.

Final Affirmation:

When I was a child, I thought, acted, and understood as a child. But now, as a Queen Mother of Civilization, I must do away with childish things.

I must become an example to the child, that the child may be guided aright.

Character Reflection #3

"Peer Pressure & Self-Validation"

Do we still do the things that we used to? Are we still succeptable to the same forces of Peer Pressure that we used to be succeptable to? Do you still submit to the lower will and influence of your friends and associates? Do you still fall victim to the same peer pressures that you used to fall for? Do you still do this? Are you a Resurrected Goddess today, or are you still of the mentally dead? What is your condition today? What is your behavior today, Blackwoman? We have to look at this.

Do you want to be a changed person for the better, or do you want to remain the same? Well are you still following the mis-guidance of your same old friends from yesterday?

Tell me something. Should a "Resurrected Goddess" be a **blind follower** of the mentally-dead so-called negro? Or should a "Resurrected Goddess" be an example of light, while serving as a **righteous guide** to the mentally dead so-called negro, leading them out of the grave of ignorance?

Who's following who? And who <u>should</u> be following who?

So, even nowadays, that you have begun to come into the knowledge of yourself, do you still fall victim to the peer pressures of those who do not "really know you", nor have a knowledge of themselves? Do you still need "their" praise and approval to feel "self"-contented or self-validated. Do you still project this "needy" character? We want to know what is your behavior today?

Come on, let's talk about this thing today. This is called "Character Cleansing". I have to keep reminding you of what we are doing and why we are doing it? We are Character Cleansing.

Now, do you still desperately "need" a pat on the head from everybody whenever you do something? Is this still you? If so, why? Do you still seek the praise of men and women, by any means necessary? Well? Are you still behaving as an attention hungry child? Hmm? Do you still "need" others to validate your own self-worth? Talk to me? You tell me.

Do you still perform, yearn and hunger for that type of attention, or is the attention of your God sufficient? Whose attention is it that you really "need"? Well, off of whose attention do you really "feed"? Who's attention is most important to you?

Do you still seek the blind approval of your so-called friends, or does the principled approval of the All-seeing All Wise Creator reign supreme in your mind? In whose sight do you really fear to be judged.

Do those peers, in whom their eyes you fear to be judged, really have any "proper sight", or "proper sense", by which to make a "properly sane judgment" of you? Do they really even have the vision of knowledge from which to make an intelligent judgment of you, and what you should do? Can a fool rightly "judge" anything or anybody? Obviously not.

Well, stop seeking the approval and opinions of such fools, and seek to know who is the Supreme Judge of your life and the Supreme Judge of all that you do. Because whomever's judgment or opinion reigns supreme in your life, is the same one whom is the guiding and validating force in your Life.

"Your" God is whomever and whatever you are submitting your will to. Your God is whomever and whatever you fear or respect overall. So, to whom, or to what are you really submitting to? Who and what is the Guide in your life? Is it the foolish peer-pressures of your friends? ...or the wise principles of your God? These are important questions. What is your behavior today?

Friends or Foes?

Are your associates or so-called friends "your" God? To whom do you submit? In whose eyes do you fear to be judged? Well, if you are still submitting to do the lower will, wishes, and desires of your so-called friends, out of the fear of what they might think of you, you have just made them Your God. You have made them gods "beside" (meaning equal to) The Most High God. You have put them and their opinions in total control of "you" and "your Life". Now, is that what you meant to do? Is this what you intended?

See, if you are submitting to do the lower will of these so-called friends, you had better ask to whom or to what it is that they are submitting to? By what principles do they function? By what principles would they persuade you to function? Do they even have "ethical principle"? Do they even have a "purposeful function"? Are they even "functioning" at all? Or are these persons just existing...taking up space on the planet?

Listen. You had better know your friends from your foes. We can not continue to blindly follow the blind. We had better cleanse this type of character quick.

As you push to rise back up into the consciousness of your true Goddess Self, there is going to be an equal and opposite force trying to pull you back down into the death of unconsciousness.

In the physical world, whenever you raise up, **The Law of Gravity** is automatically trying to **pull you back down** to the ground. In the relationship world, whenever you raise up, **The Law of Ego, Envy and Jealousy** is unfortunately trying to **pull you back down** to the ground.

Do you understand where I'm coming from? Do you understand where "you" are coming from? Do you understand where "we" are "coming from"? We are coming from the graveyard! Do you understand that? We are "coming from" the cemetery! We are attempting to raise up out of the grips of Death itself. This is where we are coming from. And that death is not going to let you go so easily. We are literally attempting to raise up out of the cemetery itself.

But, also understand that while we were buried six-feet deep in that cemetery, we made a few friends here and there. Yes, we did. You know that, if we have spent most of our life mentally dead in that cemetery over there, we must have had some friends and family right there with us. Right? Yes, the dead associate with the dead, because misery loves it's own company. Yes, the dead have relationships.

So listen, when you decide to leave that place of misery by raising up out of death, you may face a bit of a problem. Some of those people may hate to see you go! Yes, some people may hate to lose your company! You may even have to "fight for your life" to leave that deathly grave you once called your home. That is the process. We have all gone through this with family and friends.

This liberation is a process. Once your eyes become open to the light of truth, you must struggle to raise up out of that grave. Then, once you raise up out of the grave, you must "skillfully" maneuver your way over to the exit gates of the cemetery, while attempting to cross over a lot of the grave-plots and tombstones of your friends and family to get totally free. This is when you will find that those dead bodies are not as dead as you thought they were, because they will surely reach up and out of that grave to trip you, pressure you, and even try to pull you back down into the grave with them again. Oh, yes they sure will. That's right. Some of you know that this is true from personal experience.

Yes, so you made a couple of so-called friends while you were in the cemetery, and they hate to see you go. Okay. They just hate to see you go. What friend would not hate to see another friend go? Right? Right. But wait, if you are going towards that which is "life" itself, and going towards that which is "good" for you, why should they hate to see you go? Now, should they really hate to see you go toward that which is better for you? That is a good question. Are these your friends, or are these your foes? You really don't know do you?

A **friend** is one who helps and **encourages you** toward that which is good for you. A **foe** is one who **hinders and discourages you** from that which is good for you. That is the rule. That is the measure. That is the law. That is the paradigm. Plain and Simple. Simple and Plain.

So, you must determine if these persons function as your friends, or if they function as your foes? What is their true behavior and function towards you? That may be a hard question to be honest about. But, you are dealing with the extent of your own life or death here.

To encourage you toward "good", is to give you "life". Right? Right. To encourage you toward "bad", is to give you "death". Right? That is absolutely right. Either they are trying to assist you up into the "Blessings of Life", or they are trying to pull you down into the "grips of death". Plain and simple. Simple and Plain.

So, who are your "friends", and who are your "foes"? You need not to make a mistake today. If those of whom you have been used to associating with are trying to "tempt" you with the "vices", "immoralities", and "ignorance" of your old self, they are pre-meditating your murder. Yes, and it really does not matter if they do this consciously or unconsciously, because the results are just the same. You will mentally/spiritually die again, just the same. There efforts can and will kill off your new life, new mind, and new heart, just the same. They seek to bring you back to death, just the same.

I know that you think that your old friends don't mean you any harm...but that just really does not matter, because the snake that bites you on purpose, and the one that bites you by accident, can still harm, hurt, or kill you just the same. You should know this.

They will consciously or unconsciously seek to do this, because, deep in their hearts, to bring your new-found "life" back to "death" again, will make them feel more comfortable at being dead again. If they can persuade or pressure you back into doing stupid things too, then they don't feel so stupid doing the stupid things that they do. Do you understand, what I mean? These are just the bold facts.

See, if you were not so "**clean**" in your lifestyle, then they wouldn't feel so "**dirty**" in their lifestyle. If you were not so "**righteous**" in your behavior, then they wouldn't feel so "**wicked**" in their behavior. But the more "**intelligent**" you grow to become, the more inadequately "**ignorant**" they will feel. And the more "**alive**" you grow to become, the more they will feel the sting of "**death**" on them.

This makes them feel highly uncomfortable. And this feeling of uncomfortableness will cause them to react to you in either two or more ways. Either they will struggle to get up out of the grave with you, or either they will reach up to pull you back down with them. And the rest of the people will just roll over and act like they don't even see you getting up. It is true.

So, which of these is your true friend? Which of these function as your friends and your foes? Do any of your past associates even have the capacity or character to be your friend today? Answer that question. If a "friend" is described as 'one who encourages you toward the good of your own self', were they ever really your friends?

See, once you clearly and truthfully discern your friends from your foes, this "peer pressure" issue will cease to be a problem at all. This is because you automatically will not allow yourself to be pressured by someone of whom you recognize as doing harm to you.

You have to have the courage to let the dead bury their dead, and come on to walk with the living. Real friends seek to serve you life, not death. So, why would you continue to fall victim to the pressures of peers who have nothing but death for you?

If you lose their friendship, just because you do what you know is righteous, what have you actually lost? Have you really lost their friendship??? No, because how can you lose that which was never actually there in the first place?

You will have lost nothing, yet you will have gained everything! You will have gained the power of your own self-respect and self-integrity, by submitting to The Righteous Principle over the wrong doings that others were trying to persuade you towards. You will have become a friend to yourself, and you will have become a friend to Your God. Now, what better friendship is there to compare to the friendship of The God? You have no answer.

Be a Pressure to your Peers
(take your rightful place)

You must be totally clear. You must be totally clear as to who you are and what your role is. All of your former relationships must be broken up and re-defined. You must take your rightful place.

See, the only way that "the living" can be a friend to "the dead", is to assist "the dead" in getting up out of their graves. That is the only type of relationship that can be formed...and that is the greatest friendship of all time.

So, as you struggle back toward life, you can not continue to seek "the dead" out for their guidance. You can not further seek "the dead" out for their approval of you. You can not further seek to please "the dead", because what pleases "the dead" is death itself! And "the ways of death" should no longer please you, if you are a true seeker of life! You must choose life over death!

Your old relationships must be broken up and re-defined. Let's say that one more time. **Your old relationships must be broken up and re-defined!** You must now be the one to add the Peer Pressure! Instead of "them" trying to pressure you back into the misery of death, "you" press and pressure your peers to take on the virtue of Life!

While they are sitting there trying to look at you, like you the fool for trying to live right, you turn around, twist your head to the side, and look at them like they the fool for insisting to live wrong!...cause they <u>are</u> the fool!!!

Only a fool would be foolish enough to say that a "Goddess" is a fool for trying to "live as a Goddess"! And this is only because fools usually say foolish things. That is why we call them "fools". So, you had better recognize the "friends", "foes", and also the "fools" around you, so that you may establish your relationship to them accordingly.

A "Goddess Blackwoman" does not fool around with fools! She takes her rightful place and her rightful stance to lead the fool out of their foolishness! Now, what does she do? We said that, a "Goddess Blackwoman" does not fool around with fools! She takes her rightful place and her rightful stance to lead the fool out of their foolishness!

The blind can no longer attempt to lead those who have now received vision, nor can they lead their own selves. The Living are the leaders of the dead. And if you are foolish enough to seek direction from those, of whom you know are blind, deaf, and dumb, then this tells you that you are still blind, deaf, and dumb yourself....you are still dead yourself. Only a fool will follow a fool. Tell the truth now.

A "Goddess Blackwoman" can only have one type of relationship with those who are dead. She can not be a "so-called" friend to them. She can only be a "saviour" to the dead, which is to be a "true" friend and a "best" friend to those who are dead. A "life-saviour" is the "best friend" to "the dead", though they may know it not.

All of your relationships must be totally re-defined, because "you" have been totally re-defined yourself. As you continually evolve and change, your relationships must evolve and change with you. You must function in accord to each level of growth you attain. You must take "your" rightful place.

"You" be a pressure to your former peers...don't let them be a pressure to you. Add, increase, excite, and heighten the pressure on "their" conscience! Don't let them make you feel "bad" for being "good"! Make them feel "bad" for being "bad"! Don't let them drag you down, you drag them up!

Be a pressure to your peers. Re-define your relationships. You are only there to help pull them up, if they are ready to struggle to achieve the life that you have struggled to achieve. If you are not among "the dead" to "raise the dead", then you have no business being among "the dead" at all. Take your rightful place.

Make War with Your Insecurity!

Now, all of this strong charactered type of behavior may not guarantee you to be the most popular and most loved one amongst your former social circles. This may not place you as "the most favorable" in the minds and opinions of your associates. But, so what? So what? And?????? So???????

How can "the dead" have an accurate opinion of "the living"? How can you be accurately condemned in the sight of those who yet have no sight? And how can you be accurately condemned in the mind of a person, who is condemned themselves, because they have yet to accurately use their mind? This would make no sense at all, now would it?

So, just why did we continue to fall victim to this type of peer pressure, even after we knew much better? Why did we still submit to the lower will of our so-called friends? Why did we still take the opinions of a fool as truth? What has been the reason for this behavior? What is the root of this type of behavior? What is the "cause" to this "effect"?

Well, the "cause" is fear. It is the fear of insecurity which is at the root of this type of behavior. It is the lack of self-confidence that is at the root of this type of behavior.

We have insecurely feared the condemnation of other people, whether that condemnation is based on foolishness or not. We have felt good about ourselves, only after others have felt good about us first...whether they be a fool or not. We have seen ourselves as worthy of life, only after others have seen us as worthy of life...whether they be a fool or not. We have done this, being foolish ourselves. We have sought the validation of our existence from those who have yet to validate their own existence.

But, the Blackwoman with a Goddess Mind-State, is very clear on who and what validates her existence. She absolutely knows that the only "One" who has the capacity to validate or invalidate her existence is the "One" whom authored her existence in the first place. Her Creator. Her God. Who else?

In many ways, this disease of self-insecurity has totally overcome our people. This disease of low-self esteem, no self-esteem, and no self-confidence, is destroying our entire people in a variety of subtle ways that we may not immediately recognize. But yet, when a Blackwoman just simply remembers and deeply understands who she actually is, she can and will raise up out of that fatal mental and emotional dis-ease that has formerly held her down. Oh yes. This is true. This is true!

When she just simply declares herself to be a "Goddess Blackwoman", a change starts to occur inside of her. When she just verbally refers to herself as a "Goddess Blackwoman", a natural metamorphosis begins to evolve. Insecurity is slowly destroyed.

Oh yes, it is very true that just simply hearing herself referred to as a "Goddess Blackwoman", resonates the ancient memory that has been put to sleep within her...demanding that she take on the character worthy enough to carry that honorable title. Insecurity is slowly destroyed.

So, when she talks about the true reality of herself to herself, she authoritatively utters that divine title, "Goddess Blackwoman", as a call to her Highest and her Truest Self. She is calling forth that God essence of her own being. She is calling forth and demanding the highest principles and potential to come up and out of her own being immediately. She is calling her best to come up to the surface, that she may see it for herself. Insecurity is slowly destroyed.

And, once she is able to glance upon her own face to see the beauty of her own new found reflection...when she is able to bear witness to, and see the best part of her own self-character come up, out, and through her...this will cause her to grow and **restore** herself into **self-respect**, **self-worth**, **self-love**, and **self-confidence**. She goes up inside of her Highest Self to see a Goddess face to face. Insecurity is slowly destroyed.

She then becomes a witness to "the greatness" within her own Self. She then becomes a witness to "the divine potential" of her own Self. She then becomes a "true believer" in her own Self! Insecurity is surely destroyed.

Did you hear that? Did you understand that? I think maybe you should just go back 4 paragraphs to read that over and over! Those words have the ability to reveal themselves to you more and more deeply over time, as your insight develops. Living wisdom grows with you. Read that again.

After the divine Blackwoman sincerely bears witness to the true value of her own self, she seeks not the endorsement of her peers to confirm her own "personal validity", because she has now found what makes her "Personally Valid". Insecurity is surely destroyed.

She no longer seeks to be uplifted by the opinion of so-called associates and friends...because she now knows that they have not the height of mind to uplift her towards where she is going...and nor do they have the weight of wisdom to secure her once she arrives. The truth is just the truth. Insecurity is surely destroyed.

She is resolutely assured that The Righteousness and Wisdom of The God being expressed through her own being, is the rock-solid pillar of strength that uplifts and upholds "her" validity. Right? Right. Insecurity is surely destroyed!

Oh, I hope you can hear this Blackwoman. This is not entertainment! This is "science" meant to be applied! Please look, learn, listen, and do! This is a strategy of instruction. This is crucial. This takes "act"ion!

This can not help you if you do not take on the courage, determination, and persistent struggle to be "Yourself"! Yes, it's going to be a struggle! You had better fight for your life! Because this world is constantly fighting to make you other than your "Goddess" Self! You are no low-life Woman! So, stop accepting the low-life that this world is trying to heap on your back!

Get up from wherever you are, and fight for your life! Struggle to be "You"! Struggle to be a "Higher You"! Who else is going to do it for you, if you don't do it for yourself? Even God don't help those who don't help themselves!..you wouldn't either!

So, what you gonna do??? Are you going to get up and be that "Goddess Blackwoman" that you were born to be? Huh? Well? You answering to slow. What? We can't hear you? You better speak up like you mean it. Take your place, Blackwoman! Accept your own, and be yourself! Now, what is yourself? "A Goddess Blackwoman"! Well, come on.

Here is the **action-equation** of that "Goddess Blackwoman": She gets "Self-Respect" by **making herself** "Respectable" in the sight of The God. She gets the "Self-Worth" of "Self-Validation" by **proving herself** as "Worthy and Valid" in the sight of The God. What God? The God she sees face to face everyday. The God that Created her into a "Goddess Blackwoman". Think about it sister, think about it. Action-Equation.

If They did not Make You, They can not Break You!

Where is that "Goddess Blackwoman"? There she is standing on the rock solid foundation of her Righteous God. She is not standing on the wisdom of others, but standing on the wisdom of The God! She is not standing on the approval of others, but standing on the approval of The God! That's right.

She stands not on or for the respect of others. She stands on and for the respect of her God! So, when the misguided fools rebelliously withdraw their so-called respect from her...when the misguided fools rebelliously withdraw their so-called approval from her...she can not...she will not...and she does not stumble nor does she fall. This-is-because-she-was-not-standing-on-the-grounds-of-"their"-respect-nor-approval-in-the-first-place!

A "Goddess Blackwoman" is a Blackwoman upheld by the wisdom, approval, and respect of her God only. The words of the foolish can not break her. For it was not the words of the foolish that came forth to make her. She was made by the word and wisdom of The God.

Knowing this fact and remembering this fact keeps

her protected within a mind of God-Assuredness in self, and God-Validation of self. She feels no pressure but the pressure of her God guiding her on the Right Path. And even this is no pressure at all, for she rebels not this Guidance. She willingly goes where she is righteously guided.

God Allah is your only true best-friend. A friend is one who encourages you toward the good of your own self. And if The Righteous God be for you, then what mentally-dead negro can be against you? If they did not make you, then surely they can not break you. Keep striving on that Righteous Path. And be not distracted from your purpose, nor your goal. Take your Rightful Place.

Final Affirmation:

Does it profit us to seek the "praise" of fools, or to seek the "respect" of God Allah, whom is The Eternally Wise?

Treasure your own Self-respect...it's the pillar of your strength.

Character Reflection #4

"Idle-Chatter"

Do we still do the things that we used to? Do we still talk too much? Do we still run our mouths for absolutely no reason at all? Do you know what I mean? Is this your behavior? Come on let's finish cleaning up this character.

Do you talk too much, and know that you talk too much? Does your own constant chatter get on your own nerves? That's pretty bad now isn't it? Well, if your own chatter is getting on your own nerves, can you imagine the nervousness it is causing everybody else?

Do you really have "**something to say**"? Or are you just "**saying something**", because you really don't have anything to do? Surely, this is an aspect of our character that we want to cleanse, because the sound of "idle-chatter" is irritating to the ears of God...not to mention everybody else.

Yes, this is still "Character Cleansing 101". The reason that you must be so thorough, in the cleansing of your character, has to be made very clear in your mind...in order to insure that you will be persistent in your diligence to strive and endure this cleansing process. Allright?

We are attempting to set up and **rebuild a foundation of character** upon which The God can stand on and work through. All of this is to make yourself a worthy and qualified candidate to receive the wisdom, peace, power, and presence of The God within you.

This is just the same as whenever you have important guests over to your home. You especially take the time and effort to make your home respectable and clean, to receive these honored and important guests. Right?

Well, by the same courtesy, don't expect The God to come into your life and live through your character, if you have not at least attempted to make it respectable and clean, to receive "The" most Important and Honored Guest.

If you want The God to come back home, be a gracious invitation and a worthy host. Be a "Goddess Blackwoman", which is being your best self. This is the purpose for being so thorough in this "character cleansing" process. So, come on. We have 440 years of Insanity to clean-up.

Do You have "Something to Say", or Are You just "Saying Something"?
(The Power of Words)

Let us repeat the last paragraph we read dealing with this subject matter:

Do you really have ***something to say****? Or are you just* ***saying something****, because you really don't have anything to do? Surely, this is an aspect of our character that we want to cleanse, because the sound of "idle-chatter" is irritating to the ears of God...not to mention everybody else.*

Okay. Now, the question that we want to ask is, "Why is the sound of idle-chatter irritating to the ears of God?"...we already know why it's irritating to the ears of everybody else. They just tired of hearing us ramble at the mouth. Right? But your God is irritated, because your God did not create your mouth to speak "idle words".

Well, what exactly are "idle words"? "Idle words" are words that are going nowhere, words that have no point, words that have no productive purpose to them. They are just wasted words spoken in vain.

Words themselves are very important, even though we are not fully aware of that fact. But, words are actual things. Words are actual vehicles used to transfer thought from one mind to another. The spoken word can and will effect the mind and the thoughts of the listener. Words actually transfer thought from one mind to another. That is the basic understanding.

Well, this means that "productive words" that are spoken, produce "productive thoughts" and encourage a "productive mind" in the listener of those words. By the same law, "idle words" produce "idle thoughts" and encourage an "idle mind" in the listener of those words. And an "idle-mind" is the open invitation of mental-death itself.

Well, what exactly is an "idle-mind"? An "idle-mind" is a weakened and unfocused mind that is succeptable to any influence. An "idle-mind" is one that is going nowhere, a mind that has no point, a mind that has no productive purpose to it. It is just a wasted mind thinking in vain...if it is thinking at all. And it is "idle-words" that encourage an "idle-mind".

Words are more important than you know. In the beginning was The Word. And The God breathed the words of Divine Inspiration into the nostrils of Man and Woman to make each of them a Living Soul. Now, if words have that much power, what kind of words are you breathing into men and women?

If you are just breathing "idle-words", you are influencing "idle-thought", therefore encouraging an "idle-mind", therefore encouraging idle actions. We just described how an idle-mind is death. "Death" is the absence of motion and life. "Idle" is that which is absent of motion and life. Are your words producing "death" or producing "life", in those who listen to you?

Can you see now why "idle-chatter" is irritating to the ears of God? It is not so much that it just audibly irritating to the "ears" of God, but even more so, "idle-chatter" is counter-productive to the "efforts" and will of God. Idle-chatter is actually bringing "death" to minds where The God is seeking to inspire "life".

To resurrect a "dead-mind" into a "living mind", is to encourage and influence it's brains back into a positive productive thinking activity. This is to restore motion and life to a brain that was once idle, cold, still, negative, unproductive, non-thinking, inactive, motion-less, and life-less. And The God orchestrates this resurrection by breathing the Breath of Life, or Words of Inspiration, into the Mind of an individual. But anything counter-productive to this effort, is against the will of God. Do you understand this?

Oh, I don't think you truly see how this applies to everyday life yet, do you? So, let's talk about it.

Gossip Eats Away the Fabric of Community

The idle-chatter of Gossip. "He say this" or "She say that"! "**He** said ,that **you** said, that **she** said, that **he** said, that **I** said, that **you** said, the **she** said, that **they** said, such and such and such, about **me**"!!!

How many arguments and fights have you seen start with those words? How many friends, families, and marriages have you seen break apart from these type of circumstances? And if only everybody had just kept their mouths shut from this idle-chatter of gossip, there would have never been a problem in the first place. Let's look at it.

Are your words the breath of Life, or are your words the breath of Death? What are you saying to people? Why are you saying it? For what purpose are you saying it?

What type of effect are your words having upon the mind of the listener? Are you uplifting their mind into higher thought? Or are you dragging it down to the gutter of petty small minded thinking?

Are your words the cause of life, or the cause of death? Whenever you are having a conversation with "one particular person", and you begin to discuss "another particular person" who is not present in "this particular conversation", that is when you begin to invite a "particular type of danger".

You had better immediately check yourself by asking yourself these questions: *"How is this particular person relevant to this particular conversation?"* *And also ask, "What particular productive purpose is it serving to discuss this particular person with this other particular person?" "Is there some relevant constructive purpose, or is this just the gossiping idle-chatter of the foolish?"* These are your safety questions.

You must take control of your mouth and the words that it speaks. It is very powerful. It is not some vainly created creation to be used frivolously for idle purposes. It is too powerful for that.

Your mouth was created to speak the words that would transfer thought from one mind to another. Your mouth is your mental reproductive organ. It releases the seed of thought into the air until it reaches the receptive womb or mind of the listener. You had better think about that.

Once the word is in that particular womb/mind, it searches to find a firm and fertile resting place, where it can and will fully develop into a full grown idea, concept, pattern of thinking, base of philosophy, or vision of life. Your released words are powerful seeds, but are your words the seeds of Life, or the seeds of death?

This is why, when one person plants the warped seed of some negative "He say/She say" gossip, about another person, into the mind of yet even another person during the month of January....you will find that, nine months later, all three of the individuals involved will be fightin, cussin, and wishing they could kill each other, during the month of September!

And it might not take nine months! It might just take nine days, nine hours, nine minutes, or just the nine seconds it takes to dial a telephone number, before all of the fussin and cussin gets started! That one idly spoken negative warped seed has incubated, grown, and developed into a full-blown warped negative vision and negative confrontation. Another relationship ended because of the vanity of "Idle-Chatter". And in the beginning, there was just the spoken word.

Listen closely to this now. The Word is The Seed that carries the contents of your mind to another. This means that if your mind is unhealthy and ill, you can transfer the dis-ease of your mind to the mind of your listener. And if that listener's mental immune system is not strong enough or intelligent enough, their mind can become as infected and as diseased as your own troubled mind.

Then they go and breathe the ill words that they heard onto another mind...and that mind breathes the mental virus onto another, and another, and so on and so forth. Now the whole community is sick and crazy! All of this, because one person coughed their negativity on another. And in the beginning, there was just the word.

So the question originally asked was, "Do you really have **something to say**? Or are you just **saying something**, because you really don't have anything to do?"...Well, if this behavior describes you, please don't be offended by me being the first one to come on out and say "Please shut-up, because your mouth is killing us." And by now you should understand the "How" and "Why" your mouth is killing us. This is still "Character Cleansing 101".

The Art of "Verbal-Fasting"

Listen. The only way to cleanse this type of behavior is to begin "fasting". You have to go on a "Mouth-Fast". Yes, you have to abstain from speaking out-loud for designated amounts of times, until you master the control of your mouth. Yes, I am very serious about this because it works.

This is called "The Art of Verbal Fasting". The Quiet will Cleanse. Try to go for 6 hours, then 12 hours, then 24 hours, without speaking, unless it is absolutely, positively necessary. You will be surprised at how quickly your mind will feel at ease. Your mind will be at rest and at peace.

See, what you don't realize is that, all of that "idle-chatter" was not just killing everybody else listening around you, but even more so, it was feeding back into your own ears...bringing your own mind down into the lower realms of thinking. You can hear yourself louder than anyone else. This feedback produces a negative effect that initiates a deconstructive cycle. This feedback produces a negative effect that initiates a deconstructive cycle. The negativity, and the unproductive idleness of your own words, will encompass and encase your own mind under the spell of it's effect.

But, after and during this "verbal fasting", you will be surprised at how quickly the anxieties, nervousness, and stresses of your mind can dissipate, just by forcing yourself to sit in absolute quiet for a designated amount of time.

First start off with just the 6 hour "verbal-fast". Make no audible verbal sounds at all for a full six hours. It will be a struggle at first, but this is how to master your own Self-Control. Also if you want the absolute best mental results (which you do), you should go off into solitude, cut off all televisions, cut off all radios, and unplug all phones. It will be hard at first, but will be easy at last. Endure and you will see. The Quiet will Cleanse. The Quiet will Cleanse.

Even if we personally have never had problems with "Idle-Chatter", through this exercise, we can all gain more peace, purity, strength, and control of mind. "Verbal Fasting" is a constantly necessary exercise for us all. The Quiet will Cleanse.

A Goddess Speaks when Necessary

A Goddess speaks when necessary. "When necessary to do what?" When necessary to fulfill her reason and purpose. "And what's that?" Her reason and purpose is to carry out the will of The God. "And what's that?" To give life, sustain life, nurture life, and to guide life unto it's highest developed realms of potential. "Oh, now I see." Well if you see now, I guess thy will be done.

A "Goddess Blackwoman" will only speak when it is necessary to purposely communicate or to productively inform someone of something. She plants the life-giving seeded word of Wisdom in the womb/minds of her listeners. At all times, she is only seeking and speaking to facilitate the positive development of life, in the minds of her listeners.

A righteous "Goddess Blackwoman" does not engage in the silly gossip and idle-chatter of the foolish. No, you don't have time for that. As a Blackwoman on a mission, your mind is too focused for such things. Right? Right.

There is no profit in idle-chatter. So, just remain quiet in the midst of the foolish idle-chatter of others, and eventually the fools will hear the echo of their own foolishness and shut their mouths also. They will look at you and get a clue. There is no profit in "Idle-Chatter".

Idle-chatter is not a characteristic of The Wise, but "focused productive communication" is! Speak when you have something to say, not just to be saying something.

Our Creator gave us the biological ability to close our mouths, while leaving our ears permanently open. Should we take this as a hint? Obviously we need to do a whole lot more listening, than we do speaking. Don't you agree? Yes, I agree with you too.

Final Affirmation:

If you are not saying anything, please do not say anything. Thank You.

Character Reflection #5

"Emotional Thinking"

Let's deal with one of the inner most parts of our character. Emotions. Let's talk about "Emotional Thinking", and it's effects on our everyday lives.

Do we still do the things that we used to? Do we still think emotionally? Do we still react to life's situations with purely emotional responses? Well? Are your emotions still in control of you, or are you now in control of your emotions? Who's controlling who? Think about it.

Now, if you do acknowledge that your emotions are still controlling you, who is it that is in control of your emotions? In other words, who is it that stimulates and evokes your feelings, or emotional reactions and responses? Who is it that predicts and provokes your emotional behavior? Who is in charge of you? Who is in control of you? This is a very good question.

Well, in truth, whosoever and whatsoever it is that provokes and controls your emotions, is automatically in control of you. And if you do not control your own emotions, you are "out of control". Think about it. We have most definitely got to look at this thing here.

Of course this particular subject here, of "Emotional Thinking", is one of the most important out of the group.

This is because it has been "Emotional Thinking" that has led to our demise throughout so much of our lives. If we can master this particular discipline of our character, we can easily master the rest. This is a most important area of Self-Mastery.

See, you should understand that this entire world is enslaved to the "heat" of their emotions. And in the "heat" of the emotional moment, we have hastily done some drastic things, that should not have been done.

There are even whole nations and governments on this Earth, who are right now going to war with one another in the "heat" of an emotional response and reaction to one another. Many lives are being destroyed in the "heat" of the emotional moment, on every-day, in every-place, and in every-way. Let's take a look at our own life.

Blind Emotions will Drive You to Destruction

The critical question is this: Do you still submit to the "lower will" of your emotions, or do you now submit to the "higher will" of the Intelligent Thinking Goddess within you? Do "you" do what your "emotions" want "you" to do, or do "they" do what "you" want them to do? Who commands who? Which do you do? Which have you done? Which describes your character? What is your current behavior today, as a Blackwoman?

In crisis situations, do you simply react and respond, based on your emotions alone? Or do you now allow your higher intelligence to guide the force and flow of your emotions? Well? Just slow down and think about it. What do you do, nowadays? Well, what have you done before? What have you done during your own personal history? What has happened in the past situations? Stop reading for a second, and reflect. Examine the crisis situations or emotional situations of your own personal history.

A lot of times, when we really reflect on the past occurrences of our lives, we often regret the decisions that we have made, and regret the way in which we have reacted to different life situations. Is that right? Yes, this is so true. But why is this so true? Why is it always afterwards, in retrospect and reflection, that we seem to get some good sense in our head? Aren't we still that same person with that same mind? Why is it that "who we are now", and "how we think now", thinks differently and disagrees with "who we were then" and "how we thought then"? That is a key-question.

Listen to what we say to people, after those situations in which we reacted totally emotionally. We say things like, "Please forgive me, I was..I, I was just not myself that day, ...I was not in my right mind, ...I was out of control." Well, if you were "not yourself that day", who were you? If you were "not in your right mind", whose mind were you in? And if you were "out of control", who was it that was left in control?

Well, looking back, it is pretty obvious that, during those past regretful situations, our emotions were in full control of us. Right? Right. And these intense emotions "blindly drove" us into situations that we really didn't want to go into? Right? Yes I know that's right. Are you following this?

I know that you can remember the times when your emotions "blindly drove" you into making decisions that you really didn't want to make? Right? Right. Your emotions "blindly drove" you into to doing things that you really didn't want to do? Right? Right. Your emotions "blindly drove" you to destruction! Right? Right. I know that's right.

Yes, well then, this is what will generally happen, when you let a "blind" person "drive" you around. Right? Right. You know that a blind person can not "see" where they are going. They have to "feel" their way around.

Listen now. They have to "feel" their way around..."feel"..."feel"..."feel". I said "feel" their way around.

This is why an intelligent blind person will move around so slowly, so cautiously, and so carefully. They know that when you have to "feel" your way around, without the benefit of sight, you stand a higher risk of running into something that you didn't want to run into. They understand that, if they are not careful, they will either have a tremendous accident, or make a big mess. Intelligent blind persons understand this principle.

So, what would happen if there was a blind-man who was driving around, and did not even know that he was blind? Imagine that? You know exactly what would happen. Accident after accident...mess after mess...mistake after mistake...regret after regret. Right? This is what would happen.

Well, just wait a minute now. Hold it. This "accident after accident...mess after mess...mistake after mistake...regret after regret", kind of sounds a lot like the trail of our lives, doesn't it? Doesn't it? Come on, you can be honest.

When you turn around and look back at "where" you have traveled, and "how" you have traveled thus far in life, do you see this trail with "accident after accident...mess after mess...mistake after mistake...and regret after regret"? Yeah, well me too. You are not in this by yourself, and neither am I.

I must admit that I can see the same trail behind me too. I'm surprised that we haven't already met before now!...since we have been traveling on this same road for so long? But it's okay, it's okay, because we are now looking for an exit off of this worn-out road. We are looking forward to a road much less traveled than this one. Okay? Okay.

But looking back now, we have learned the valuable lesson that: You can generally expect "accident after accident...mess after mess...mistake after mistake... and regret after regret" to happen, when you let a blind-lady drive you down the road of life...especially a "blind-lady" that does not even know that she is blind! She is especially dangerous! She "boldly" moves around, to her own demise! Boldly wrecks her life, like she just know she knows what she's doing! Too blind or too proud to ask for some help. Does this sound like someone you know? Does this character sound familiar to you? Well, it should.

Now, of course you already know that this "blind-lady" is representative of nobody but you. You do know this, don't you? Who else did you think? Come on, stay with me now.

This "blind-lady" is describing you and me. The word "blind" means "the absence of vision". So, there are many of us who are mentally and emotionally blind, but do not know it. And this is only natural, because when a person is "born" blind, they do not know that they "are" blind until someone tells them that they are in-fact blind. Otherwise, how would they know the difference? Think about it.

See, our blindness is not that of the "physical eye", more so than it is that of the "mental eye". Our mind itself is an "eye" that "sees" and "analyzes" things in the range of it's own "focus". Yet, when our mind is covered and befogged within the cloudy mist of emotions, our mind's eye can not see a thing. We are just as blind as blind can be blind. Pay attention now.

See, these Misguided Emotions are blind "feelings", that can only "feel" their way through life's situations and decisions. And when we boldly, plus blindly, move throughout our lives based on just "feelings" alone, we are bound to make accident after accident...mess after mess...mistake after mistake...and regret after regret. And this we have done. This we have done.

This we have done, while trying to "feel" our way through life. We "think", "act", "make decisions", and "make choices" based on impulsive emotional "feelings", as opposed to "thinking", "acting", "making decisions", and "making choices" based on the "higher reasoning" of intellectual mental "sight". We have used our emotions to "feel" our way around, instead of using our mind's mathematically logical intellect to "see" our way around. This is what has caused much trouble.

Surely we have been traveling throughout our lives as blind persons in the cloudy mist of our own emotions. Don't know quite where we've been. Don't know quite where we are. Don't know quite where we're going. Wherever the next stimulated emotion takes us, there we go. That's true.

Wherever the next provoked emotion takes you, there you go...but there you go where? You don't know do you? How could you know? You ain't driving, your emotions are driving you! You just riding as a passenger! Well, I hope you got a seat-belt, an air-bag, and some paid-up insurance, cause you going for a ride sister! Ups and Downs! Ins and Outs! Left to Right...back where you started from!

If you do not take the control to drive your own emotions, your emotions will blindly drive you into brick wall after brick wall, gutter after gutter, and ditch after ditch! This leaves us damaged, embarrassed, and stuck in repetitive rutts for most of our lives. You know this is the truth.

Who is Driving Who?
(Which Part of You, is Driving You?)

Listen, listen, listen. I don't want you to think that "Emotions" are bad things. "Emotion" itself is a very, very, very, necessary thing, and a very good thing when properly harnessed, controlled, and guided.

I know that we have just discussed how our emotions have negatively driven us to do many destructive things in the past, that we may even still regret to this day. But it is really not the emotion itself that caused problems for us and others, it was the way in which we reacted and responded to the emotion that caused problems for us and others.

We may even attempt to place blame, by saying that our emotions drove us to do something wrong, but who should've been driving who in the first place? That is still the question. And, either way it goes, you are always the one who is driving you. You can not escape that responsibility. It is always "You" driving "You". There is nobody involved but you.

Now, the deeper question that we want to ask is, "What part of You was driving the vehicle, at the time of the accident?" Whenever you have found yourself driven to destruction, which part of you was it that drove you into that destruction? Which part of you was it, that was in the seat of control at that time?

Did you know that there are two parts of the one "you" contained in the one "you" simultaneously? Just like there is a left-brain and a right-brain to make up your one brain, there is a "higher mind" and a "lower mind" to make up your one mind. Both minds can think, but one thinks lower thoughts and the other thinks higher thoughts.

The "lower mind" can produce the lower thoughts of frustration, anger, jealousy, envy, and false pride (or arrogance), which are really all different forms of the same insecurity of fear.

But basically, that "lower mind" thinks with the desires of appetites and the passions of emotions. It "sees" very dimly, if it sees at all. While, your "higher mind" thinks with the process of logical reasoning and with the intellect of calculated wisdom. It "sees" much more clearly. In other words, one mind is kind of childish, immature, uncontrolled, and wild, while the other one acts like it got some good sense.

Okay, so now that we know that there are "two parts" to our "one mind", which part seems to be running your life today? Which part should run your life today? Which mind "should" steer, guide, and drive the controls of the other mind? Should your emotions dominate over your intellect? Or should your intellect dominate over your emotions?

Well, why is it that so often our Lower Emotional Mind is driving our Higher Intelligent Mind? This is like getting in your car, and sitting on your head. Can you really expect to not have an accident driving around like that in a moving vehicle? I think not, and most sane people would agree.

But if we never even knew that there was a "higher mind" and a "lower mind", ...if we never knew that we were driving through life upside-down sitting on our heads, or sitting on our intellect, ...if nobody ever told us that we were boldly and blindly wrecking our lives, ...how would we ever know any better? How could we know? So, don't blame yourself for that past behavior.

Although today, this understanding will make you responsible and accountable for your present and future behavior. A new understanding automatically requires a new behavior. So, let's thoroughly understand this thing.

What is Emotion?

"Emotion". Look at the word. "Emotion". Let's break that down into it's inner components for a better understanding.

"Emotion" = E-motion = Energy-motion = Energy in motion = "Emotion". Think about it.

Your "**emotion**" is a reservoir of purely intense combustible energy stored within you, which can be stimulated by any number of factors internally or externally. This energy of emotion can manifest in many different levels or volumes of intensity. Plus it has many different outward expressions and forms depending upon the particular stimulus that is stimulating it.

"Emotion" is the source and manifestation of "Energy in Motion". It is "The Fuel". It is "The Power". It is that which gives "Mobility".

Emotion is That Fueling Energy that Empowers and Moves The Intellect. Intellect is That Focused Intelligence that Guides and Directs the power of Emotion.

Every Organism, or organized creation, has an Energy and an Intellect. The Energy and The Intellect must be separated, distinguished, organized, and prioritized in their complimentary relation to one another.

Look at the sperm cell of life. This organism has an Energy and an Intellect. It has a Tail and a Head. The Tail is the source of Energized Mobility. The Head is the source of its Directed Intellect. The Tail helps The Head meet it's Destination, and The Head helps The Tail meet it's Destination. This is teaching us something.

The Head cannot get where it needs to go, without the Mobilizing Energy of The Tail, and The Tail cannot get where it needs to go without the Directed Leadership of The Head. They are no good without each other. An undirected tail is bound to crash, while an unmoved head is powerless, purposeless, and non-potent. It is like a thought with no action...un-realized and un-verified, as if there was never any thought at all. This is teaching us something.

The importance of both The Head and The Tail are equally important to the purpose of Creation or Life, in a horizontal balance. But in order to fulfill this purpose of Creation, or Life, one must submit to the other in a vertically prioritized order to properly function. This is teaching us something. Just come on, follow this.

The Tail must be smart enough to get behind The Head and push, while The Head must be smart enough to get in front of The Tail and lead. That is the Complimentary Relationship that functions on purpose and toward objective. This is teaching us something.

They both must submit to the nature and purpose of their Creation, lest total chaos is all that they achieve. And it is this achievement of chaos, that we know all too well, as our tail is leading our head and our head is following our tail.

The Emotions and The Intellect are equally important to the Purpose of Creation. And they can only fulfill this purpose when they are put in their proper and natural place.

Take your Personal Intellect and mount it up on top of your Personal Emotional Energy. Your Emotional Character may currently be like a bucking untamed wild-horse full of energy, but with no planned rationally intelligent direction to travel. So, it will take the persistence and the skill of your Intelligent Character to train, tame, reign, saddle, and harness that powerful Creation. You must be a skilled rider, guider, and driver, lest that powerful Energy in Motion will buck you right off of it, to fall on your butt again. And I know that we are all tired of falling on our butts throughout this life.

But, once you Master the Skills of a Guiding Intellect, that Energy in Motion will submit to you. Your Emotional Character will organize, prioritize, and submit to your Intelligent Character. No longer will your Emotions and Intellect be at odds with one another, they will be as One Mind and One Will. Perfect Compliments. Perfect Balance. Perfect Reciprocity. Perfect movement. Perfect Peace.

And, once this matrimonial Unity is formed within you, you will become a fluidly functional Human Being. There will be no thing that you can not Accomplish...together. There will be no Creation that you can not Create...together. There will be no Destination that you can not Travel...together There will be no Goal that you can not Meet...together.

You will then have the power and ability to will (or wheel) your thoughts into action, and your ideas into reality. The Creator gives a Goddess the power to create also, once she exhibits the disciplined ability to intelligently control that which is already created.

In order for you to be given the freedom to create the Life that you want for yourself, you must exhibit the responsibly intelligent Discipline, of Emotional Self-Control. Freedom is gained through Disciplined Maturity. Discipline is no enemy to freedom. It is the means to that freedom.

If there would be any life situation whatsoever that would potentially provoke you to react purely emotional, just ask yourself "What would God do in this situation?", and you will thereby know exactly what a Goddess should do.

Your God does experience very strong emotions, but is not driven nor led by them...God leads them instead. A Goddess does the same. Don't let your blind-emotions recklessly drive you to do anything, lest they drive you right off the cliff.

Distinguish, Harmonize and Prioritize the Two Characters in your One Being. Place the Energetic Mobility of your Emotions under the Guiding Control of your Intellect. And Peace will be Achieved. Peace will be achieved.

Final Affirmation:

Whosoever controls your emotions, is thereby in control of you.

Yet, if you control your own emotions, you will thereby have Self-control.

Character Reflection #6

"Posture of Pride"

Do you still do the things that you used to? Do you still carry yourself in the manner that you used to? Do you still maintain the same limp posture as before, back when you believed that you were nothing more than a "nigga", "negro", and "colored person"?

Do you still maintain the same posture as before, back when you believed that you were nothing more than a "worthless", "life-less", "purpose-less", "class-less" slavewoman? Is this your posture?

What does your body language reflect about your current state of mind? What is your body language saying to the world? What is your body language saying to yourself? What mentality is your body language reinforcing within your own self?

Do you still carry a "pittyful-posture"? Or do you hold your head up high and walk with a straightened back, now that you understand that you are the "Goddess of the Universe and Queen Mother of this Planet Earth"? You do understand that, don't you? Oh, you do huh?...well show and prove it.

Does your body language manifest a **"posture of pride"** or a **"slump of shame"**? Well? That's right go ahead and sit-up straight, I see you. How else should a righteous "Goddess Blackwoman" carry her divine self? Hmmm?

You know how she should walk. She should walk as if she has the backing of The Supreme God, because she does! Her back should be **firm** and **straight**, to reflect her **affirmed mind** of God-confidence, as she walks the **straight path**! Her head should be held **up** high, to reflect the **high** and heavenly **state of mind** that **lifts up** her total being! Right? Right! We are talking about that Mighty Goddess Blackwoman!

But wait. Do not take this "Posture of Pride" out of it's proper context. Again, this-should-not-manifest-in-the-form-of-arrogance! No! No! No! No! That will not work. That would be totally incorrect. No. Arrogance can find no resting place within the heart of a true "Goddess Blackwoman". Let's talk about this thing.

True Pride vs. False Pride

A true posture of "self-pride" is by no means a posture of "arrogance" toward others. No, that is not what we are teaching here. If you are egotistically arrogant, you actually have no real self-pride, nor self-love.

This is because that disease of arrogance is rooted in self-hatred...the deep inward hatred of self. Arrogance manifests from a person who feels so ashamed and fearfully insecure about their real self, that they feel it necessary to put up a false front for everyone else, including themselves. Many think that arrogance comes from one who is "too proud" of themselves, but on a deeper level we can uncover the rooted "cause" to this "effect".

At a deeper level, arrogance is a "false-pride". Arrogance is really a "low self-esteem" attempting to hide itself. Arrogance is really a "self-hatred" also attempting to hide itself. The behavior of arrogance is really a "deeply rooted fearful insecurity" attempting to disguise itself. Arrogance is really a "false-pride" attempting to conceal it's true feeling of shameful insecurity. Yet, this "arrogance" can find no resting place in the heart of an awakened "Goddess Blackwoman". And this insecurity disguised as arrogance can find no real hiding place from the eyes of the wise.

A Blackwoman with a Goddess Consciousness, has no need to put up an arrogant front, because she is a "truly" proud woman, that has something to be "truly" proud about. A Goddess Mind State, produces a self-assured confident woman of a "faithful understanding". She is assured of the power and potential of her own individual being, yet she fully understands that this same peace and power belongs to all of the righteous!

A "true pride" fosters a sense of "gracious humility". Look at the term "Gracious Humility". A "Goddess Blackwoman" deeply understands that it is only by the purest grace of The God...She is. And, by this same mercy and pure grace...Anyone Can Be!...everyone should be! She is agreeably clear in her understanding about this. She is no vain woman.

The Love of Your People is not "Selfish Vanity"

So, your posture of peace and power should never offensively nor arrogantly "provoke" any of your Black Sistas to feel ashamed, envious, or jealous of you. No, there ain't no love in that. But rather, after seeing you in your radiantly glorious upright stature, they should feel proud to be Blackwomen, and therefore be inspired to let your righteous character be in them!!! Yes! This is exactly what should occur.

They should see and feel the glow emanating from you, and thereby be inspired to start being their own Original Divine Goddess selves again too! That's right! And you should do everything that you can to assist them in their efforts. That is called **LOVE** for self and kind! What is it called? It is called **LOVE** for self and your people.

We don't want you to get crazy and think that you are going to keep all of this light and life-giving wisdom all to your own selfish self! Ain't no devils allowed here! Knowledge and wisdom ain't your personal possessions! We were all raped of a "Knowledge of Self" back on that wicked plantation! All of us!

This fruit of Righteousness and Wisdom belongs to all who seek it. And those that try to hide it to themselves, will lose it. In fact, the very selfish act of trying to hide it, means that you have lost it already.

So, don't you be trying to keep the light all to your little crazy self, when you see your people dying right in front of you everyday. Do you understand what I'm saying to you?

You know how we can get sometimes. We get a little money, and then we start hiding it. Or, you know how we sometimes get a new outfit to wear, but we don't want to tell nobody where we got it from, because we don't want them to buy one...afraid that they might look as good as us, or better? You know? And that selfishly ugly attitude makes you look the ugliest already.

See, being a childish and foolish people, we can sometimes behave the same way when it comes to the riches of knowledge and wisdom...you don't want to show others where you learned from...afraid that someone may end up smarter and wiser than you. Silly. If they do excel further than you, maybe they can then turn around and teach you! Let them return the favor.

Don't get crazy and think that God is your personal tutor. Only devils conceal knowledge to themselves, just like the white racist slave-master works night and day to conceal knowledge from us. Don't be the devil. Don't be the devil. Don't be the devil. Don't-be-the-devil. Be The Goddess, that is your true nature. Spread your mental riches generously, but "wisely"...but "wisely"...but "wisely".

Be wise. Be wise when feeding your people

knowledge and wisdom. Don't try to shove a whole steak down a baby's throat, when you know the child only has one tooth to chew it with. Nurture your people generously, patiently, and wisely. I have to say these things because you know... we really don't have too much good sense as a people. At least that is the case for right now, so we have got a lot of work to do.

Be a wise Goddess. "Share the light and life" that God Allah was merciful and beneficent enough to share with you. "Share the blessings" with those who would come drink of God's wisdom. That is **LOVE**. That is **LOVE**. That is **LOVE**. Be a **Goddess**. Be that **Love**.

Be the love of a **"Truly Proud"** Blackwoman, that is positively and confidently assured that she has something to be truly proud about. We don't need the fearful insecurity of a **"Falsely Proud"** arrogant woman gripped with shame. Arrogance can find no resting place here. Be the strong love that is your nature, and have something to truly be proud about. And when you truly have the courage to get to know the depths of yourself, you will truly have that in which you can truly be proud of.

Righteousness begets righteousness, and wickedness begets wickedness. If your self-confidence becomes selfish-arrogance, it will eventually come back on you. Yet, if your self-confidence becomes a collective-love, it will also eventually come back upon you as well...and that is a good thing. That is something to be proud of.

Final Affirmation:

Even though a Goddess walks with her head up high, she makes certain that her feet never steps on anyone down low.

Even though her back stands firm and tall, she keeps it flexible enough to bend-over and lift-up the down-fallen sister or brother.

...for a Goddess understands that the only thing in between high and low, is the merciful Grace of God Allah.

Character Reflection #7

"Indecent Exposure"

Indecent Exposure. Indecent Exposure. Indecent Exposure. Come on now, you know we just have to talk about this subject here...especially today in these present times. It's time to do some serious Self-Reflecting.

Listen now. Do we still do the things that we used to? What do you look like in public today? What does your "outer image" reflect about your "inner image" today? If your mind-state truly has changed, has the state of your outward appearance changed also?

Do we still dress the same as we used to? You know what I mean. Do you still dress as that cheap, worthless, low-class type of woman, that your slavemasters taught you to be. Or do you dress as a righteous Spiritually Awakened Goddess Blackwoman of priceless value? How do you see yourself today?...as a "cheap woman"?...or as a "woman of priceless value"? Come on, let's take a look.

Well, what type of clothing do you keep in your wardrobe? Do you still wear cheap and provocative clothing that reveals your privacy to the public? Do you still wear all of that tight-fitting type of clothing? So tight, that it used to cut-off all of the blood circulation to your Brains, before Your God came and woke you up and put some sense back in your head? Are you still wearing this stuff? Huh?

Are you sure that you are this woman of priceless value? Are you sure that you believe yourself to be a "Goddess Blackwoman", as your God has declared you to be??? Maybe you still believe yourself to be that cheap promiscuous hoarish type of woman that your slavemaster swears that you are. He swears that you are this. Oh yes...you didn't know?

He swears that the Blackwoman is really nothing but an animal in heat...and this he loves. That's why he is always trying to get next to you, because he is the real animalistic beast in heat. Yes, that's what I said. Oh, so you didn't know? Yes...well we will just have to talk about this more, in a few minutes. You will remember. You will remember it all.

Can a devil dress a Goddess?
No, not Nowadays.

But listen, now. Let us take a look at this thing...you and me, me and you. Let's look at it. So, let me ask you: Do you still wear that clothing that exposes your body indecently? Well? Well, really, what in this hell is even considered to be indecent "these days"? I don't even know if there is even still any such thing as a word called "indecency" anymore. I don't even think the word is even used in today's vocabulary.

As crazy as a Blackwoman has been made to be these days, she would be doing good, to just not come out of the house stark-naked! I must sincerely say that it is a damned shame what has been done to our minds. There should not be a day that goes by, that a tear does not fall from our eyes, over the sickened condition of our destroyed people. We really need some help. We need help.

Look in the mirror at yourself today Blackwoman. Just look. Come on now. Come on. What are you doing to yourself? Is it the mission of a Goddess to try to show the world the beauty, shape, and form of her physical body, more than it is to try to show the world the beauty, shape, and form of her divinely wise mind and her spiritually pure heart? Well? You tell me? Go ahead, you can answer. What's your answer sister?

Here...we are going to finish asking these questions. Do we still do the things that we used to? Look in this mirror at yourself. Look down for a second. How high is that split in your mini-skirt? Hell, does a mini-skirt even need a split? Well, just wait a minute now, does a Righteous Blackwoman even wear mini-skirts??? Does that represent The God? You tell me? What do "you" think? What is "your" answer?

Look up for a second. Wear is your neckline? Is your chest indecently exposed? Is your back out? How is your blouse cut? Is your blouse made of a "see-thru" sheer type material? Why do I even have to ask that question? A "see-thru" blouse...what kind of sense does that make? You let somebody sell you a "see-thru" blouse.

Let me ask you something. Why would you purchase a garment to cover your body, and expose your body at the same time? What the hell type of sense does that make? If you can see thru it, why would you want to put it on in the first place? Huh? If you are going to be naked, just be naked! If you are going to put some clothes on, put some clothes on! Just as crazy as can be!

Are you sure that you want to be a Righteous Blackwoman? Are you sure that you want to be of the Righteous???...I don't know if you like all of this questioning too well....now do you? Too bad! And, don't punk-out trying to close this book, running from your truth! Sit on down here and read the rest of this. You ain't got nothing better to do. Oh no you don't! What can be better than getting some good sense back in your head? Nothing!

You should be tired of letting this world make a fool

out of you! And if you ain't got sense enough to be tired of being made a fool, I'm tired enough for all of us! I'm tired of watching fools manipulate other fools into more foolishness! Do you understand what I'm saying???

You are just going to have to come face to face with the reality of yourself today...for better or for worse. You Coming-Up today Blackwoman, from wherever you are! I'm tired now...I'm just tired. The patience is drying up.

We are just asking questions today. Right? I know...I know...I know! I know that you do what you want to do, you don't have to tell me. I know. I know that you are a free and independent woman that does as she pleases. I know. You can take that attitude off of your face. I know that don't nobody run you but you. I know. You can stop rolling your neck. I know. It's your world. You running it.

It's still all up to you. And it is always going to be up to you. Of course...you are always going to do what you want to do, but you just need to ask yourself one question. "Why" do you want to do what you want to do??? "Why" do you want to do what it is that you want to do??? Huh?

Why do you want to parade throughout the streets with your body indecently exposed??? Just, why do you "want" to do this??? What is your purpose??? What is your motive??? That is a good question, and you don't have a good answer do you? No, I didn't think so.

Now, come on and walk through the rest of these questions with me. We ain't finished yet, so don't try to put this book down. You can't get rid of this...I'll start talking to you in your conscience!...in your mind...in your brains! You can't put your brains down! Well, hell, maybe you can. That's why you crazy now. Anyway, let's finish. Now, come on and read this book.

A Walking Peep-Show

Well listen. Is your dress or skirt pulled all up around your thigh, or is it decently placed below your knee?

What are you doing Blackwoman? Are you trying to show somebody something? What are you doing? What's going to happen when the wind starts blowing, and you got on that little-bity tight skirt? What's going to happen when you try to sit down? What's going to happen if you have to bend over to pick up something off the ground? Well?

You know what's going to happen! Your business is going to be all out in the street for everyone to see! Right?! Right?!? Your little naked business is going to be all out in the street, fool. Yes, we are going to talk frankly with one another!

You squeeze your grown body in those little baby clothes, and your business is bound to be out in the street! Or is that the way you wanted it anyway? Huh? Maybe this is how you planned it, with your crazy self. Maybe it is your intention to dress like your "business" is "in the street". Yeah, that's it! Maybe you just a modern-day "businesswoman"! A businesswoman! Is that what it is?

Maybe you just a "street merchant", and you just advertising your "goods" and "services"? Right? Maybe you just into "stocks and bondage"...on Wall Street, Hall Street, and whatever other street you can generate some business on???

Is that what it is sister? Maybe you trying to conduct your own little personal peep-show??? Uh-ohhhhhh...Uh-ohhhhhhh. What you frowning for? You don't like this, do you? You got a problem with this, don't you? Well, if "you" don't appreciate this, let me ask "you" another question.

Is it just that you would want to purposely attract a Man to you simply based on the external outer dimensions of your physical body? Huh? Answer Blackwoman!

Are you just a piece of meat on display? Just a big lump of flesh for men to lust after? Is that all that you are worth? Is that all that there is to you? Are you that simple??? Are you that shallow??? Are you that cheap??? Is that it? That's the only way you can attract a Man??? I said, answer me, Blackwoman!

Well hell sister...if that's the case, if you are that small minded, then maybe you need to just go ahead and dress like a prostitute to get a Man??? Just maybe you don't have the "Beauty of Personality and Character" enough to attract a Man otherwise? Maybe that's it. Maybe you just can't attract a Man with the attractiveness of your Mind. Yeah, I understand. If you ain't got no brains to show, then just show your body. What the hell?...might as well. Right? Right? No...Wrong! Wrong!

I keep trying to tell you that you ain't never gonna be happy as no "fool". That is the whole point of this book. I said that, you ain't never gonna be happy as a "fool". You will not be happy at all, because it is not your nature to be a "fool"! Do you hear me? You know that you want a Man who will be attracted to the Beauty of Your Mind, Your Heart, and Your Character? This is what you want, right? Well? Talk to me, I can't hear what you saying? What do you want for yourself?

Female Hoars attract Male Hoars

What is your thinking today? What is your state of mind? Why would you simply want to attract a Man to you based on the exteriors of your outer physical body? Why would you hold yourself in such "cheap" value and "cheap" esteem? Are you even conscious of what you are doing?

Listen to this real good, sister. If you do attract a Man to you, simply based on your **"body"**, how long do you really expect this man to be with you? You know that there is always going to be some-**"body"** better than yours! And as soon as some-**"body"** better comes along, your so-called Man, has gone along with some-**"body"** else other than your own **"body"**! Now you left feeling like a no-**"body"**. What a shame.

And what kind of "so-called" Man would be attracted to you, if you are dressed like a "cheap-hoar"???

Come on, we gonna talk about this today! We gonna talk real straight about this today! We need some straight talk...you and me...me and you...we and us! We talking now.

The question was: What kind of "so-called" Man would be attracted to you, if you are dressed like a "cheap-two-dollar-and-fifty-cent-hoar"??? Huh? The truth is that no "Man" will be attracted to you! No! You will attract no "Real Man"! You can only attract that which is the reflection of your own self! That is just the Law of this Universe.

So this tells you that "Female hoars" can only attract "Male hoars"!!! If it is a "cheap-two-dollar-and-fifty-cent-Male hoar" that you are looking for, then you just keep right on advertising for one!!! You hear me? You'll get one sooner than later!

I know what you saying, "I ain't no cheap two dollar and fifty cent hoar!!!"...yeah, well, why you trying to dress like one? Huh? So, what you trying to get all mad and upset for? Don't get mad at me! I didn't dress you! What did I do? Don't be frowning and looking all irritable at me. Hell, I would be irritable too, if I had all that tight gripping polyester cuttin-me all-up round-my behind!!! You know you just crazy, don't get mad at me.

How could I have offended you? Did I under-price your value, according to the current street exchange rate or something? Is that what I did?...maybe it's "two-dollar and 'fifty-two'-cent hoar" or something? Maybe I just mistakingly under-rated your street value or something? I'm sorry, I just don't know too much about these things in detail. All that I do know is, if you got a problem with this, that is being said, then you got a problem. I can't offend you more than you are offending yourself. You know???

I mean, Blackwomen have been made so Devil-Damned crazy today, that I have even seen you dress your little 5 and 6-year old daughters in all of this slut fashioned clothing!!! And you wonder why all of these precious little girls are being sexually molested by their sick Fathers!!!

Sick Uncles!!! Sick Brothers!!! Sick Cousins!!! Sometimes it is because their "Sick Mothers" are too damn silly to protect their own daughters, because they are too damn busy acting a damn fool they self. And a young girl's life is ruined forever!!!!!!! Raped, assaulted, and destroyed before she even gets a chance at life.

You better listen to me Blackwoman!!! I don't give a damn, how much of a fool you want to be yourself, in your own life, but you had better have some decency and some sense enough to protect your daughters, from all of these strange Men you got coming in and out of your house! This goes for family and friends alike! You just don't know the secrets that so many women are walking around with today, dying on the inside. Protect your daughters, and protect yourself. Put some damn clothes on your naked behind.

Maybe you just picked up the wrong book or something. I thought that the title made it clear enough. This book just ain't about keeping you in the same ignorant image and likeness that your slavemaster has put you in. No, no, no. I think that maybe you may have mis-read the cover.

Yeah, I know we talking. If this book offends you, then you just picked up the wrong book. You may have been looking for **"Reinforcing the image, the character, and the irresponsibility of the Two-dollar and fifty-two-cent Hoar Blackwoman"**. Is that the book you meant to pick-up? Maybe you should just forget that you ever even started reading this. Huh? I guess this just ain't the book for you, cause God ain't no pimp, and this "Goddess Blackwoman" ain't no "hoar"! So, now what? Now what?

Can a devil dress a "Goddess"? No, not nowadays. But, can a devil dress a two-dollar and fifty-cent hoar? Yes, all day long. And when I say "devil", you better know that I am not talking about no spook under the ground, or no spirit floating around! No, wake-up and get some common sense in your head today beloved Blackwoman.

I'm talking about your lust-filled slavemaster walking around on the top of this ground! You know, that same one who purchased boat-loads and boat-loads and boat-loads and boat-loads of Black female slaves to be his live-in personal prostitutes, all for his nasty, sweaty, evil, lustful, demonic pleasure! Don't you remember this? I said, do you remember this Blackwoman!?!? Do you!!!???

He raped you every day after day, and every night after night, as his live-in "physical property"! Do you hear this??? Do you remember this? It is suppressed in your genetic memory! You didn't even know that you were suffering today, from the suppressed memory of being sexually assaulted time and time again. You are more of a victim than you consciously know. And now today, he persuades you, encourages you, teaches you, conditions you, and trains you to voluntarily dress like the cheap-hoar that he has degraded you to be...all day long!!! This is a shame! This is Our Shame! This is the shame of an entire Nation.

So listen, if you are offended, this is exactly the book for you! This is for you. This is a personal love letter from me to you. I love you, so I'm gonna tell you the truth about yourself. I'm your best friend...the best kind of friend that you will ever have! The others won't tell you, cause they don't really care about your well being. But "I" love you! And I know that you can do better, and I know that you will do better, once you get some sense up into your head. I know this.

I'm going to let you know that you are much more valuable than you think that you are. I'm gonna help you to help yourself, back into a sane state of mind, just like somebody helped me...and is helping me. I'm loving you because somebody had the heart enough to love me, and begin to lift me up and out of foolishness!

You no longer have to be your slavemaster's hoar, Blackwoman. You just don't have to do that anymore. Let this truth make you free of that. You are a Free Woman today! Free to be your natural "Goddess Self". And you are not mad at me for talking to you straight like this. Oh, no you are not. No, No, you aren't upset with me. You already know you crazy and need some help, so you love this truth deep down in your heart. You know you love me, cause you know I'm just trying to love you, with your crazy self. Now, take that frown off your face, and let me see a smile! Yes, I love you too. I do.

You know that I haven't told you nothing but the absolute truth. You know that I have not advised you wrong. And if you also know, that if you were Truly Sane and Healthy in the mind, you would have never had any problem with this truth. You would have had no problem. You know that you are suffering from a degraded state of mental and emotional dis-ease. You know this to be true.

You know that it is pure insanity to dress and act like a **"cheap-hoar"**, while at the same time expecting to get treated like a **"first-class woman"**. That is insanely irrational thinking. It's okay though. After all that our people have gone through, we all just about crazy up in here. But, you have to agree, that it is pure insanity to dress and act like a cheap-hoar, but at the same time expect to attract a respectably decent Blackman. The world just don't work like that.

Have you ever really thought about these things? Have you ever really thought about why you just can't seem to attract any decent Men? Have you? Well what do you plan to attract a decent man with, other than the principle of "decency" itself? **You can only receive for yourself, what you make yourself worthy enough to receive.** You can only get back what you are giving out.

A strong Blackwoman automatically attracts a strong Blackman!!! And a divine Black Goddess automatically attracts a divine Black God! Yes, and if you are dressed as a Prostitute, you are automatically going to attract some fool that thinks he's a Pimp! That is the law of The Universe. You attract what you are. You attract what you are.

Now what is it that you have been attracting to yourself, by walking around half-naked? Hmmm? Well? Yeah, I thought so. You still "reaping" exactly what you "sowing"...and you always will reap what you sow. Always.

Are You Crazy and don't Know it? ...most likely you really are.

Think about it, think about it. Look outside your window today. We have lost the good common-sense of sane thinking and rationale today. Brains just dead and mind just malfunctioning today. Imagine a sister walking around half-naked, but yet at the same time, she is all upset and got an attitude, because everywhere she goes the brothers are howlin, whistlin, and hangin all out the car-window foamin-round the mouth. And she has the nerve to be upset? She has the nerve to be upset! Upset???

This is just like walking around with a T-bone steak hanging out of your back-pocket, and then gonna have the nerve to get upset because a whole pack of dogs start chasing you around the block!!! Now, what kind of sense does that make??? Hello?! Hello?! Are you still there? Or, is your brains just completely off the hook??? Insanity!!! Insanity!!! Brains just dead! Mind just malfunctioning! How you gonna have the nerve to get upset???

Think about this society in which we are living today. Here is a woman walking down the street, with a little pistol, or a can of mase in her purse, to stop a would-be rapist from attacking her. But yet at the same time, she is walking down that same street in a pair of skin-tight shorts, cut-off all the way up to her crotch, a see-thru sheer blouse, and with a low-cut strapless lace bra on up under that!!!

Now, would somebody talk to me, please?! Is this the budding symptom of a mental-disorder, or is it just full-blown lunacy?????? God! Help! Us! Please! Cause! We!

Have! Lost! Our! Minds!!!!! Brains just dead. Mind just malfunctioning.

Listen, I know that if you are reading this book, most likely you are not going to get that crazy...I hope...I hope. I said "I hope", because I have seen some sisters walking around in African Kente cloth mini-skirts, with their thigh hanging all out the split talking about, "I'm just being free and natural like back in Africa, the Motherland." Silly.

Yeah, well this ain't no "Motherland", you living in the "Devil-land" right now!!! You mess around and get your little naked self snatched-up, and there won't be no Tarzan or no Cheetah to come save your foolish self!!! Don't you lose the rest of your mind. We just as crazy, as crazy, can be crazy. Brains just dead. Mind just malfunctioning.

The Queen has to be a Queen

Look, let's get back to the point of this discussion. The bottom line point is this. Don't say that you can not possibly be "fashionable", and be "righteous" in your style of dress at the same time. Don't say that...That's not true. I understand that the beautiful "Queen" has to be the fashionable "Queen" of beauty and all of that, but you have to be creatively righteous in displaying that Goddess beauty.

You can be fashionably modest in your everyday dress. Yes, you can. Yes, you can. Where there is a sincere righteous will, there is always a sincere righteous way!

Yes, yes, yes, I know that you are beautiful and you want everybody to know that you are beautiful too, but indecently exposing your physical body does not show any of your beauty. It shows the ugliness of your degraded mind-state.

Exposing your physical body is only attractive to lust-filled beasts. But, covering or clothing yourself protects you from the violence of these lust-filled beasts in the streets of this depraved society.

Your conduct, your character, and style of clothing, can and will "protect you" from criminal attack...just the same way as your conduct, your character, and your style of clothing can and will make you a "likely target", mark, or candidate for criminal attack. That is true...read that again and think about it. Dress to protect yourself, while displaying the beauty of your illuminated "Goddess" mind-state. Clean. Orderly. Neat. Natural. Modest. Radiant. Respectable. Beautiful.

This is the true beauty that is attractive to true Blackmen. This is the true beauty that is attractive to Gods. Beasts attract beasts, and Goddesses attract Gods. Fools attract fools, and Queens attract Kings. You will get what you ask for. It is all up to you.

Now, if you still think that indecent-exposure is the only way that you can attract the eye or attention of a Man, maybe you just don't know how to dress properly? Okay, maybe that's the problem. Maybe you just aren't being creative enough? Maybe you just don't have any style or something? But, walking around naked is no excuse....that is just the style of a desperate fool. Are you a desperate fool? No, I didn't think so.

So, since the Queen just has to be a Queen, be a Queen. Be fashionable, be beautiful, and most of all be sensible at the same time. There are many fashion options and choices to accent your natural beauty.

This Goddess Blackwoman used to be The Measure of Illuminous Beauty all throughout the Earth. Yet, where is your beauty today? By what measure do you determine beauty today? How do you dress yourself today? How do you see yourself today? What image do you project today?

Your House of God
(Is this the Residence of Royalty?)

Constantly reflect and reprove yourself, for your

own self. Nobody has to see you more than you. Your own self-reflected beauty has a profound inner psychological effect. Radiate that life and vitality back unto yourself.

You don't want to still wear those same lifeless dead colors, like most anglo-saxon european women, do you? Reflecting death back into your own face? Or do you want to wear illuminated, bright, living, vibrant, African colors like orange, yellow, or white? Of course, if you are a righteous Blackwoman who is full of spiritual light and life, any color will look vibrant on you.

This is real, and this is self-healing psychology (science of the psyche). The clothing that we choose to wear, all the way down to the color and pattern, has a deep psychological effect upon us everyday. It's true, think about it.

For example...Have you ever noticed that the entire spirit of a "house" can totally change, just with the simple change of a new decor? Have you ever walked into a house that looked so dead, depressing, and lifeless that it seemed to drain the energy right out of you? Yeah, me too.

But, have you also noticed that when a new family moves into that same house, the whole spirit of the house can change? I would see that same house later on, with new bright paint, brand new wall-paper, new floors, new furniture, new light fixtures, clean windows, green plants, etc., etc. And the same house that once projected "death", would now project "life"! The same house that once "drained" energy from people who came into it, now inspires the people with new "energy" and "vitality"! All of this because of a "New-Decor"!

Well, what about your own personal house...your physical body...your house of God? Do you project "Life" or "Death"? What is your "interior decoration" and your "exterior decoration"? Who lives in your house today, a negro, a slavewoman, a temptress, or a "Royal Queen-Goddess"? Does your house look like the Residence of Royalty? Who lives there?

Do you project "life" or "death"? Listen, you know exactly what I'm saying. The point is to look "vibrant", not drab or dead...look "vibrant", not wild or flamboyant either. Balance. Clean. Orderly. Neat. Natural. Modest. Radiant. Respectable. Beautiful!

Balance! Clean! Orderly! Neat! Natural! Modest! Radiant! Respectable! Beautiful!!!!

Just remember that you represent the righteous presence of God Allah in the person of you! And, of course, don't try to say that I am trying to encourage you to go and cover yourself, by wrapping all up in a bed sheet looking like a Mummy or nothing. No, you are not going to get out of this thing like that. I'm just encouraging you to dress like you got some "good-sense" in your head. No. As a matter of fact, dress like you got some "God-sense" in your head!

You don't want to be that low-life, class-less, Cheap Woman that your slavemaster wants you to be. You don't want to be the Degraded Shame of Your People! You want to be the Uplifted Glory of Your People! Civilized. Beautiful. Queen. That's You.

Final Affirmation:

The Radiance of your True Beauty begins within your "heart and mind".

Strive to Beautify your inner-self, then watch it's glow radiate to the surface of your physical, and beyond.

Yes, and just as surely as you allow this Beauty to emanate out from you, it shall surely return unto you. Goddesses attract Gods. And Queens attract Kings.

Character Reflection #8

"Grooming Habits"

Since we are on the subject of beauty already, let's ask some more questions relevant to this same subject matter. This is still self-reflection, self-character-cleansing, and self-image-reconstruction.

Do we still do the things that we used to? Do you still have the same old personal grooming habits? Do you always strive to maintain a neat and clean appearance about yourself? Self-reflect.

Do you maintain this neat and clean appearance at all times, even when you are all alone in the privacy of your own home? Self-reflect.

Personal Grooming Habits are Personally for You

Remember that this is not simply about looking pleasant for others, more so than it is especially about looking pleasant for yourself. Let's say that again. "Remember that, this is not simply about looking pleasant for others, more so than it is especially about looking pleasant for yourself"!

"You" have to make a good impression on "you"!

Your own self-reflected image will directly affect your own personal self-esteem, self-respect, and self-confidence. "You" have to make a good impression on "you"! This is why you must strive to maintain a neat and clean appearance at all times, and not just when around the company of other people.

You are always around the company of yourself, and you should be more worried about how "you" see yourself everyday...because **it is your own self-opinion that will make your life or break your life**. That self-opinion is powerful! More powerful than you may know, but you should know how powerful. **It is so powerful that it conducts the spirit and course of your entire life**. The Self-Opinion.

When you **"look good"** to yourself, you will **"feel good"** about yourself. When you **"feel good"** about yourself, you will have a **"good attitude"** about yourself. When you have a **"good attitude"** about yourself, you will bring forth **"good actions"** from yourself. And when you bring forth **"good actions"** from yourself, you will receive **"good fortune"** back unto yourself.

Just the same, on the other hand, when you **"look bad"** to yourself, you will equally **"feel bad"** about yourself. When you **"feel bad"** about yourself, you will equally have a **"bad attitude"** towards yourself. When you have a **"bad attitude"** towards yourself, you will equally bring forth **"bad actions"** from yourself. And when you bring forth **"bad actions"** from yourself, you will equally receive **"bad misfortune"** back unto yourself.

This is just the mathematics and science of Psychological Law. It is unescapable. The Self-Opinion, puts all of this into motion. So, keeping that in mind, we really want to strive seriously at maintaining a **"Neat and Clean", "Groomed Appearance"** at all times, but most especially when we are looking in the mirror at our own selves. This is still even so much more important than we may realize.

See, **whenever you just slightly glance at self, you are automatically forming a negative or a positive opinion about your own self, consciously or unconsciously.** You are automatically gaining or losing respect for your own self at all times. And it is this foundational base of a negative or positive "Self-Opinion" of our own self-perception, that directly shapes the condition and events of our lives. Just think about it. And read that point over and over again. It is just that important.

Does Your Reflected Self Display Chaos or Order?

So, let's look in the mirror right now. Let's look to see if we are looking at the image of a person that we can "Respect and Admire".

No matter who you are in life, or where you are in life, every person innately respects "Cleanliness and Orderliness". Even if we do not care to make our own selves "Clean and Orderly", we innately respect that which is "Clean and Orderly". Cleanliness. Orderliness.

Now, the question that we are dealing with is; when "you" see "you", can you respect and admire what you see about "you"? Do you see Cleanliness and Orderliness looking back at you, when you look into the mirror? Look carefully into this mirror.

Examine your personal grooming habits. Look at your self-reflected image. Do you see "Chaos" or do you see "Order"? How is your "face"? Is it "clean"? How is your "hair"? Does it look "neat"? Is it "groomed"? Is it always "freshly" braided, twisted or locked? Is it "freshly" and "neatly" arranged? Is your "natural" freshly cut? Does it stay freshly faded?

Or do you still happen to maintain a straightening perm? If you still do, does it look freshly permed? Do you have poker-straight pieces sticking out of your hair-doo? Is your perm old? Do you have new growth? What's going on?

Do you have Blackfolks hair, at the roots, and whitefolks hair at the ends? Make up your mind, either have it all of the way permed or all of the way natural, because the two don't mix! Integration does not work! Separation is the only answer! Look at your society. Is this society really the great integrated "Melting Pot" it professes to be? The only thing that has "melted" away is your good-sense.

You still Wanna Be a White-Woman?

The Great "Melting Pot" means that everybody in this country, who is non-white, has to melt down their culture and moral standards, to assimilate the culture and standards of European Caucasians. That is America's real "Melting Pot". Everybody in this Pot trying to melt, except for whitefolks.

That is why most of you don't feel that you are beautiful, unless you are reflecting some european-caucasian beauty standard...with them blue contact lenses pushed all up in your eye. I see you. It's no wonder that you can't see "reality", if your eyes ain't even "real" themselves. You got more Blonde Streaks in your hair, than Marilyn Monroe. What the hell is wrong with you? You know that's the truth.

We just as confused as we want to be. Just go to the mirror and look at yourself. Look in the mirror and talk to that woman. Talk to her. Look in that mirror, and ask yourself a question. Say: "Self...excuse me, but what the hell is wrong with me?" And your Honest-Self is going to answer back saying, "You still wanna be a White-Woman. That's what's wrong with you."

Wait now, and let's talk about this other thing. Let's talk about this "temporary permanent" you got whipped up around your head. Yes, you know we had to talk about this. Don't try to run now. You probably sitting in the Beauty

Shop reading this book right now. And, I want you to be courageous enough to really ask yourself, "why" are you paying all of that money to get a "temporary-permanent" in your head? 30-days of pretending that you a white-woman.

You know, it is quite possible that you look real silly, to the rest of the peoples of this World. You know? I mean, to want to look like a white-woman so bad, that you would chemically alter and disfigure your own body to look like another woman. Damn, now that is deeply seeded low self-esteem and self-hatred. There is nobody else on the Planet that does that...nobody else that hates themselves as we do.

If you started seeing a whole group of white-women, who started pinch-braiding, twisting, and locking their hair in African hair styles...dying their hair Black, or putting Black streaks in their hair-doos, and buying Pretty Dark-Brown contact lenses for their eyes, wouldn't you look at them a bit strange? I mean wouldn't you think that maybe they would need some counseling or something? I mean wouldn't you suggest that they really needed to find themselves?...and be themselves?

Wouldn't you think it to be a bit mentally and emotionally unhealthy, for these Grown White-Women to be running all up behind you like children, trying to be like you in everyway? That behavior would be a little "off", don't you think??? Yes, well I agree with you. And now, you know how the Whole World looks at you, Blackwoman in America. Still a slave to your Master. Yes, our condition is shameful.

Yeah, I know what you saying: "I ain't trying to look like no white-woman, this just the style that I like." Well, why do you like that particular style? "Cause...I just do, that's all. Plus, men like my hair like this." Well, if your man wants to run his fingers through some stringy-hair, you just tell him to go find him a real white-woman!...instead of trying to make you into one! Trying to make you into his fantasy white-woman! You falling for that? You going for that sister?

Is the only way that he can appreciate your beauty, is to pretend like you are that white-woman, that he really wants to be with? You better make sure he wants "you" for "you", and not because he couldn't have what he really wanted. You sitting up there burning your scalp with chemicals trying to be his fantasy white-woman. You tell me, who is more of the fool, you or him? I think it's a tie.

I thought you said you wanted to be a "Goddess Blackwoman". Why do you still have that perm whipped all up around your head anyway? Hmm? I'm talking to you particular sisters, who have supposedly been "mentally awakened" for a while now. The average sister just didn't know no better until now, but what is "your" problem? You supposed to have had some sense for a while now, so what's wrong? You still wanna be a white-woman too, huh? After all the wisdom that you have been exposed to, you know you need to be ashamed of yourself. Still ironing your hair. "You" shouldn't even need to be involved in this conversation, but you sit down and listen too.

Do you think that God made a mistake with "your" natural hair? Do you think that your Creator just "mistakingly" gave you that strong wooly hair? I guess you do, since you've been spending thousands of dollars trying to correct that "mistake" every since you've been born. Right?

Well, do you think that God made a "mistake" with the hair of Black Jesus too? You know that your Bible said that his hair is like lamb's wool too? Did you know that? Do you think that Black Jesus gets a perm every thirty days or so, while the disciples wait outside the beauty-shop? Does The God get a touch-up every two weeks? What do you think? Imagine God walking down the street looking like "super-fly"? Can you imagine that? Well, look at you.

The God doesn't want you to get your hair "<u>fixed</u>" because it was not "<u>broken</u>" in the first place! How can you call yourself, "going to get your hair done"? Your hair is "done" already! Save your money Blackwoman. Don't contradict yourself.

What kind of psychological damage are we doing to ourselves, walking around trying to look like, and imitate the murders and oppressors of our own People? **We would rather chemically alter and disfigure our own appearance to look like those who have treated us with such evil, rather than to be in the natural image and likeness of The God that Created us.** Brains just dead. Mind just malfunctioning.

We are truly in need of some serious Mental Sanity. And our needs are now being fulfilled. Always maintain a neat and "natural" appearance. God did not make a "mistake" with his beautifully wooly hair, or your own beautifully wooly hair, so don't you make any "mistake" either.

• • •

Remember that, whenever "you" look at "you", you do not want to see an image of chaos and disorder staring back at you. The Goddess Blackwoman is one seeking an Orderly Peace within herself as well as without.

Whatever you see without, will reflect back within...and whatever you see within will reflect back without. That is a law constantly at work.

If your body is The House of God, then treat it as such. Strive to bring Cleanliness and Order to both your Exterior and your Interior, that they may bring it back unto you. Personal Grooming habits are personally for you.

Final Affirmation:

"You will only feel as good as you look, and you will only look as good as you feel!"
"Self-Image is a Master-Key towards Self-Love."

Character Reflection #9

"Orderliness"

"Orderliness", "Orderliness", "Orderliness". Do we still do the things that we used to? Do we still maintain chaotic and messy surroundings? Take a look around.

Yes, look up and around yourself for a second? Just look at the place around you. Do your surroundings and atmosphere still reflect the confusion and chaos of your old mind state? Or do you now maintain and reside in an "orderly" and "peaceful" surrounding that reflects the "organized" and "peaceful" mind-state of the Goddess Blackwoman that you are? What do your surroundings say? Chaos or Order?

I know that in the last Character Reflection #8, entitled "Grooming Habits", we talked about the importance and the need to have a neat, clean, and orderly appearance to our own selves, but what about the condition of the area around ourselves? How important is that? What effect does that have upon us? ...our Image? ...our Character?...our thinking?

The Science of Impression

Well, our atmosphere may actually have more of an

effect upon us than we think. The Image and Character of your atmosphere or surroundings, can and will have a direct effect (or direct "impression") on the Image and Character of your own self, and your own thinking. This Psychological Law works the same way in every case scenario.

Take this for example. Whenever you look upon that which appears to be in a "chaotic" disarray, it will form a "chaotic impression" upon the thinking of your mind as well. Just the same, whenever you look upon that which appears to be in an "organized" and "orderly" fashion, it will form an "organized" and "orderly impression" on the thinking of your mind. It is true.

This is just as, whenever you glance upon that which appears "beautiful" to your eyes, you derive a certain internal pleasure, enjoyment, or peace. By the same law, whenever you glance upon that which appears "repulsive" to your eyes, you derive a certain internal displeasure, discomfort, or disturbance. See, it all carves a deep "impression" into you, whether you are conscious of that fact or not.

The amazing thing about this fact is that, these reactive feelings of pleasure or discomfort, actually come from chemical and hormonal releases into your brain and bloodstream, that are being stimulated just by what you visually "see"! Isn't that something? Everything that you place your eyes upon produces a chemical reaction in your brain and body, that impresses an actual emotion or feeling upon you.

The lens, pupil, and retina of your eye will visually pick up an outside pattern, and chemically make an "impression", of that pattern, upon your brain...just like photography. Photography is nothing more than a process of light, chemicals, and impressions. So likewise, your mind can take disturbing pictures or beautiful pictures, depending upon how the scene of your surrounding atmosphere is set.

The scene of your surroundings can and will have a direct bio-chemical, mental, and emotional affect (or "impression") upon your behavior, and the behavior of others.

For example, this is true of when people enter into a very elegant hotel. Their behavior automatically modifies to become very "civil" and "respectable", because they have just entered into a very "civil" and "respectable" surrounding. And of course you know that when the surroundings of a place is very "disorderly" and "unattractive", people's behavior in that place will eventually become the same. "Disorderly" and "unattractive". Oh, yes this is very true. This is simply the Science of Impression.

What do your Surroundings Say?

So, now that we understand the laws of the Science of Impression, what impression do our usual surroundings impress upon us and others? What is the Image and Character of your surroundings? Do they reflect the character of cleanliness, orderliness, and righteousness? Do your surroundings say, what you want them to say, back unto your own conscience? Do they impress upon you the images that you want impressed upon you?

How is your home? Who lives there? Does it look like the place where a Queen lives? How is your personal bedroom? Who sleeps there? Does it look like the place where a Goddess sleeps? If you walked into your home as a stranger that had never been there, what kind of person would you assume lived there? What would be your impression? Good Question.

What is it that our atmosphere is saying about us, as a person? Is it telling an accurate story? If our atmosphere does not tell the true story about who lives here, then we should immediately re-create the atmosphere all around us, to tell the true story about who really lives here! "You" set the scene! "You" are the writer, director, and the actor of this story! "You" set the scene! "You" create your own world around you!

The Act of Creation:
To Bring Order out of Chaos

How do you create Your Own World around you? Well, what is the original method that Your Creator used to create this World?

Your Creator is constantly creating this Universal atmosphere, by the method of "bringing order out of chaos". Evolving the world to higher stages of organized perfection. "Bringing order out of chaos". And this is the same method by which we are to create the atmosphere of our own lives...our own worlds, or our own life. Just follow this now.

Your pattern of thinking is always going to be the center of your life, or your world. And the condition or state of your life or world, will always revolve around the condition or state of your thinking. Your state of thinking produces your state of Life. This is why we want to bring the thinking of our minds out of a former state of "chaos" into a present state of "order", by which every aspect of our lives can and will follow suit. That is the process, the protocol, and the plan. Okay? Do you follow?

Now, with that understanding, we want to find all methods by which we can get our minds together. And I submit to you that, the cleaning and organizing of our outside atmosphere directly helps us to clean and organize the internal thought processes of our minds. So, "Orderliness" is what we strive for, inside and out.

Really, this act of "bringing order out of chaos" is the entire purpose and function of our lives. Are you listening? Did you hear that?

Listen now. I said that, **the act of "bringing order out of chaos" is actually the entire purpose and function of**

our lives. We want to bring that which was formerly in a state of "nothingness" into a state by which it can now be considered "something"...of value ...of worth ...of purpose. Think over that.

"Orderliness", "Orderliness", "Orderliness". To bring "order" out of "disorder". That is the point to this discussion. That is the point to this life. Even our ancient symbol of the Pyramid represents this point, of "bringing order out of chaos", or the process of creation itself. "Actualizing" that which was once only in a state of "Potential".

Look at the Great Pyramids. Here you have an arrangement of many individual stones, that have now been scientifically and meticulously organized, into a mathematically aligned structure of "order". It is now put into a creation that has been structurally engineered by the precision of perfectly exacted measurements; when at one time, that same Pyramid was once nothing but a "chaotically" scattered pile, of various pieces of jagged rock and stone. In it's former state of chaos, it was considered "nothing", but in it's present state of mathematically Disciplined Order, it has now become a wonder to the world!

Okay, well listen. We are not talking about pyramids, just to be talking. This symbol of the Pyramid is giving you and I the Instructions of Life itself! We are to bring ourselves and our lives out from a chaotically scattered pile of insignificance, into an organized state of Divine Wonder! This is our Daily Instruction, our Daily Prayer! Let Us Make Blackwoman!

You are already "something", that was once a pile of "nothing"! Your anatomical creation is already just a pile of dust that has been magnetized, organized, and gathered, around a Supreme field of Electrical Intelligence, that called you into existence and keeps you in existence as we speak! You are mud gathered around a spark of sunlight!!! That's what you are. A walking Planet. Just stop and think about that.

Now that you know who you are, and what you are...go and create your world in your Image and Likeness. You go and stand up directly in the center of your life; and "You" be that Supreme Field of Electrical Intelligence, that authoritatively calls all of those chaotically disorganized pieces of your life together, into an Organized Functional Creation...an Organized World...an Organized Sphere of unified particles, that smoothly rotates and functions by the light and law of your spiritually disciplined thought. "You" be that spark in the center that holds it all together! Holding together The Order of Your Atmosphere, or Your Sphere of Atoms! Your World...your Heavens...your Earth...Your Life!

Listen now, in conclusion of this discussion, understand that, even though the state of your atmosphere should always reflect the state of your mind, the truth is that, the state of your atmosphere already reflects the state of your mind. All that we have to do is to take a good look around us to get a good look at what is going on inside of us. It is merely a cycle of reflections and impressions.

Yet, if you want to change your mind, change your atmosphere. If you want to change your atmosphere, change your mind. One will make an impression on the other. Put it all in Order. Put it all in your Self-Control.

Final Affirmation:

God's mission is to resurrect the life out of death, and to spark the light out of darkness, which is to bring the Order out of Chaos.

The Peace is where you bring it, and The Heaven is where you make it. So, be...and it is.

Character Reflection #10

"Effective Communication"

Now that we have been thoroughly looking at ourselves and our atmosphere, let's now begin again to listen to ourselves. We have "Looked", now let's "Listen", and we will "Learn". Come on! Come on! Wake-up, sister. Don't fall asleep now. We have just a little more to go. We are going to repetitively drive these points into our brains, until they get branded into our thinking and behaviour. We want to be made new all over again.

Do we still do the things that we used to? Do we still speak in the same manner? Does the manner of our speech reflect our newly purified heart? Let's take another listen.

Does the **Tone of Your Voice** represent someone who is **Full of Life** and rejoicing over the fact that **The God is Alive** in their life and their being? Or does the tone sound cynical, sarcastic, pessimistic, and doubtful? Take a listen.

Are you sure that you are bearing some witness to the light and life of God Allah? Has the Reality of God really entered the Reality of Your Life? If so, shouldn't you be happy? Let's examine this thing.

Effect-of-Communication
(Effective-Communication)

"Effective Communication" is our subject. Therefore, we want to examine the "effect of our communication". What "effect" do our words have? When we speak, do we create the desired "effect" from which we were motivated to speak the words in the first place? In other words, do we get our point across?

What is the effect of your communication? In social situations, sit back and listen to your own self talk to other people. What kind of words do you speak? Is it that every word and statement out of your mouth is a negative one? When you speak, are people left feeling **dragged-down** and **depressed**? Or do they feel **encouraged** and **inspired** by your positive words of optimism? Take a listen.

Of course, as a "Goddess Blackwoman", you are to bring good news to a people who have only known hopelessness and despair for so long. Hopelessness and despair comes from the fear of an "unknown", "unseen", and "uncertain" future. But, you are one who is to bring "optimism", or in other words, bring a far reaching "optical-vision", which is a wisdom that sees far beyond temporary despair. This provides a faithfilled hope for an assured future.

An "Optometrist" is one who corrects the vision of his patients. "Optimism" comes from looking at the world through the perfected vision of God. And the God's Words are spoken from that position of "optimum-vision", to "reprove", to "inform", as well as to "uplift" the people's "outlook" on life, by getting them to see the world through God's eyes. "Optimisim". "Optimisim".

The God takes his clear word, and rubs it in the eyes of his blinded listeners, that they may see correctly again. That is the optimistic effect of God's communication. So, do you speak today as The God speaks? Do you speak "optimistically"? As an uplifted Goddess yourself, of course you should speak words that uplift!

You are Your Words, Spoken and Unspoken

Just your very presence alone, is supposed to uplift, and inspire hope for your people. You become The Word. A "Goddess" is to be The Word and The Wisdom of The God, animated through a material being in person.

You are always going to be the manifestation of whatever "words", "concepts", and "ideas" that reside and swirl in the base of your brains, as well as whatever "motivating intentions" that reside in the root of your heart. You are The Word. You are always going to be the product of Some Word. Good Word or Bad Word. Yes, we are talking here today.

Examining the "outer" effect of your communication, tells you a lot about the "inner" you. This is because you are the words that you speak, and those same words are you. You therefore want to make sure that the words that you speak are of good effect, and of good intention to those that hear them (which means yourself and those to whom you are speaking to).

Use your words for the purposes to improve, inform, or to uplift. Discipline the **tone of your speech**, the **content of your language**, and the **motivation of your intent**, when you speak. You should always be the silent third party, monitoring over your own communication and general behavior. Take a listen.

"Purposely Direct" Your Words

Here let's continue to examine and monitor our past and present communication habits. Now, is your language **polite** and **courteous** today? Do you say things like, "Thank-You"? "You are welcome"? "I'm sorry"? "Yes sir"? "Yes ma'am"? "My brother"? "My sister"? Do you speak this way? Should you speak this way?

Yes, you should speak this way. You should give this respect even to persons who have not yet learned to respect themselves, that they may eventually learn to do so. Your speech can actually serve that directed purpose...to encourage self-respect. It truly can.

Well since you know when to be respectfully **humble** and **polite**, do you know when to be "politely" **firm, strong, resolute, and authoritative** in your speech? Can you do this without becoming overly emotional? You don't have to roll your neck all around to make a point about something. Just be calm, honest, direct, and straight to the point. Tell the truth calmly and directly, to get the best results from the effect of your communication.

"Directly". Yes, tell the truth "directly". If you have something to say, just say it. Don't beat around the bush wasting your time and somebody else's time too! Speak directly and honestly! Honesty is still the "best" policy.

You don't have to sugar-coat your language or play little childish games with people. It ain't worth all of that! Just speak directly! There is no God but The One God! And, it feels so good to just have One God to please, instead of curbing your words to please everybody else's little fragile egos. Be considerate of others, but be real. Be "considerate" of others, but be "real". Balance. Balance.

Effectively communicate. Speak. Are you so shy, that we can barely hear you speaking? Do you speak too softly? Do you speak-up!? I can't hear you! What? What? Speak-up! Let the word be heard! What? What'cha say? Speak clearly! What? Effectively Communicate.

We know that you have something to say Blackwoman. Go ahead and direct the intended purpose of your words. Implement your language in a most confident, articulate, and professional manner. Practice, Monitor, and Master your communication skills. Confidence. Sincerity. Clarity. Effective.

They say that the "eyes are the windows to the soul".

Yet, the words from your mouth are the windows to the state of your mind. Say what you mean, and mean what you say. Remember, "You are your words...spoken and unspoken".

Final Affirmation:

"Speak the uplifted Words of The God", in sincerity...and you will eventually "Become the uplifted Words of The God", in sincerity.

"...And The Word became Flesh."

Character Reflection #11

"Productive Living"

What is "Productive Living"? "Productive Living" means to "live productively". What does it mean to "live productively"? To "live productively" means to diligently spend your time, in and on the purposes of producing something which is beneficial to the quality of life itself.

But, are we now spending our time productively, or do we still do the things that we used to? How well do we **manage our time** today? Do we even manage our time at all? Is it that we are still **wasting our time** away? What are we doing today?

Well, let me ask you, to see what you think about yourself personally. Are you focused in your life? If you do consider your life to be focused, what is it that your life is focused on? That is a good question. Do your daily, weekly, and monthly activities benefit you toward that focus?...benefiting you mentally, spiritually, economically, or intellectually? Are your daily, weekly, and monthly activities those that will propel you towards your life's goals and aspirations? Wait a minute. Have you even set any life-goals and aspirations? You can't plan to get anywhere in life, if you have not sat down and planned where you want to go. What's your destination, your goal? Where you going, Blackwoman? What you doing, Blackwoman?

Look at the daily activities of your life today. Do you spend quality focused time? Or are you still trying to "play" and "party" all of the time? Who are you today? What kind of activities are you doing everyday? Remember...Do you need to be **educated** or **entertained**? You answer. What do "you" think? How much leisure time does a "Blackwoman on a mission" have?

How much leisure time does Allah God have? I know that on the seventh day he rested, but that is because he was working all of the six days before. He had a right to be tired, now what you acting all tired about? What have you done? What are you doing? Well, what are you going to do?

God don't sit back all day watching "As The World Turns" on television! Your God stands up to determine "How The World Turns", through the tele-visionary capacities of his Infinite Mind!!! Do you understand what is being said to you??? Now, that ought to give you a clue of what a Goddess should do! God Consciousness is God Consciousness.

Remember, that your children are watching you, Queen Mother Blackwoman. But what are you showing them? They already know how to waste time, beloved! So, be focused in your actions or activities. If the activity isn't benefiting you in any way, then just stop doing it! If it is not serving the purposes of your goals, then what is the point of wasting your time and energy? What's your purpose?

Your God lives, moves, and does everything for a **productive reason**, and a **productive purpose**. That is focus. That is an example for you and I. Everything that we do, should be for a productive reason and a productive purpose, otherwise we should immediately disassociate ourselves from it, since we are trying to be a productive people. Right? Don't you think this is best too? Sure you do, I know that you are a "Blackwoman on a mission". A "mission" is a planned objective to reach a certain goal in a certain amount of time. Mission.

"However you spend your time, is how you spend your life." Your life is nothing but a segment of Time itself. "Life-time". So, what are you living for? What would you give your life for?

Well, you are already automatically giving your life for something. Whatever you spend the majority of your time doing, is exactly what you are living for...exactly what you are giving your life for. You should know that. You should know that.

So, what are you giving your life for? Think about it. And what was your life given to you for? Think about it long and hard. You think about it long and hard until you come up with a concrete, rock-solid foundational answer by which to live the rest of your days.

Don't wait until your last day, to turn around and look back at the days of your life, to think of what you would've, could've, and should've done. Look at your life right now, and determine what you should, could, and will do today, tomorrow, and so on. Self-Determination.

Final Affirmation:

God created "all" living things on purpose, including you.

So, are "you living" on the purpose for which "you" were created? Invest your time productively.

Character Reflection #12

"Fulfilling Relations"

Do we still do the things that we used to? How do you deal with your relationships nowadays? Do you still treat male/female relationships as sport, fun, play, amusement, and entertainment to past the time? Do you? Do you still play the little games that you used to?

Does the relationship, in which you are currently involved, reflect the consciousness of your renewed mind-state? Are you and your mate on the same path, morally, mentally, and/or spiritually?

If not, then why are you still currently involved in this same relationship? What are your reasons? Are your motivations pure, true, or wholesome? What could you possibly seek to gain from a situation such as this, when the purpose of a relationship is to forge unity, not to foster opposition? Ask yourself these questions.

If you are not currently in a relationship at all, then what type of relationship is it that you seek, and for what reasons? Do you even give this much thought to your relationships? Do you even know why you should, or even "if" you should, be this concerned about your relationships, or potential ones? Why should a Goddess be so concerned with this subject matter? What does all of this have to do with her Image, Character, or Responsibility as a Blackwoman? Well, these are very good questions...very good questions. So, let's talk about it.

The Value of The Male/Female Relationship

This particular subject, of the male/female relationship, may have more of an importance than we are currently aware of. Yet, we should understand that a Blackwoman with a Goddess Mind-state, must be very concerned about her "relations", because it is her "relations" that produces the civilization itself. And the "quality" of that civilization which is produced, will largely depend upon the "quality" of the male/female relationship that produces it. That is real. Don't just pass over these words, I want you to think.

As a Goddess, you should know that alongside The "Mother of Civilization", stands The "Father of Civilization"; and as that Mother, you can not "properly" Mother Your Nation, if you have not the "proper" Father by your side, to encourage, support, and strengthen you toward your responsibilities, as That Mother.

A Goddess Blackwoman understands that a "Queen" can not be a "Queen", if her mate is anything less than a "King". And she also understands that her "King" can not be a "King", if she is anything less than a "Queen". One supports and upholds the other reciprocally and equitably.

A Goddess has a Deep Reverence and a Profound Respect for the male/female relationship, because she deeply recognizes it's eternal sacredness. She knows that the relationship between a Man and a Woman is the balancing of the Universe itself...the very foundation of all that there is...the complimenting masculine and feminine energies of all Science...therefore all Creation. The Sacred Union. A Goddess understands this. She does.

Although, because of the majority of us being previously disconnected from this knowledge and understanding, we have been very irresponsible in dealing with our previous relationships. In most cases, we have very hastily, naively, indiscriminately, and carelessly chosen our mates for all the wrong reasons, potentially setting ourselves up for a lifetime of mistakes and misery. Is that right? Yes, that is very right. You know it is.

But right now today, from the advantaged position of new consciousness in our lives, we must look at this issue of "Fulfilling Relations" from the awakened eyes of Knowledge, Wisdom, and Science. This is because, as The Mother of Civilization, that male/female relationship is the very medium through which you create the world around you. The male and female expressions of energy/electricity are the two components by which you create and sustain the energy of life itself. The Balance.

This does not only and simply refer to the "physical" procreation between the male and the female, but rather to the "mental and spiritual" levels of procreation as well. The Mother of Civilization is not just simply one who physically gives birth to children, but rather she is one who gives birth to "Minds". She is the womb of "Minds", and the womb to "States of Mind". And it is these "Minds", and these "States of Mind", that determine the "State of the World" around you. Listen.

She not only multiplies reproductions of herself physically, but she does this mentally/spiritually as well. Her "nature" is the portal and doorway thru which minds are nurtured and passed on to elevated places of existence; or even the portal and doorway thru which minds can be dragged down vice-versa. Think about that. Just listen.

This means that everything from the state of the **Family**, to the state of the **Society**, to the state of the **Nation**, to the state of the **Planet**, to the state of the **Universe**, passes through the portal of a Womb, a Mind, a Doorway. Yes, she is the Mothering Factor that influences it all. And it is also the particular male/female relationship that she chooses to involve herself with, which will influence and determine her ability to birth that civilization into a "constructive" state, or even into a "destructive" state. Yes my sister, you are dealing with more power than you ever knew you had in your possession.

"No such thing as a No-good Woman"

The Mother is kindred to The Earth. And, in her state of neutrality, the Mother Earth will bring forth the fruit of whatever type of seed that we place into her soil to bring forth. And if it is a "poison seed" that is cultivated into the Mother Earth, that "poison seed" not only brings forth a "poison fruit", but it even "poisons the Earth" into which it was planted. The Earth was good and wholesome at first, until it was contaminated. Are you listening? Now, what did we say all of this for?

This is an example of why our honorable brother, Elijah Muhammad, told the World that "There is no such thing as a no-good woman." No such thing. He went on to say, "Wherever you find a no-good woman, there was some no-good man that made her that way." Think now.

This teaches us that the neutrality of The Mother Earth, The Mind, The Womb, is originally pure and virginous, until its contents are "spoiled" by an interaction with a "soured outside influence". This spoiling effect has been the case with the Earth, Mind, and Womb. Outside influences of sour intent have spoiled them all. Do you follow what is being said? You have to think about these things in parallels. Slow down, and keep up.

Listen, as a result of being "spoiled" and "soured" by these outside influences of ill-intent, there has come the time in which the Neutral Earth has moved into a more actively-aggressive nature and/or consciousness, in order to protect and sustain it's own life, by expelling all things that interfere with it's own purity of life and natural state of peace (neutrality).

A Time of Separation

Today, Your Earth is now actively ejecting contaminants and contaminators from it's soil, surface, and atmosphere. The Mother Earth is doing this by moving into a "state of consciousness" that distinguishes, discriminates, and discerns what good elements it will continue to receive, and what bad elements it is now forced to reject. This Earth is now in a "state of judgement", consciously investigating and deciding a judgement upon all who seek to stand before her.

It is a time of Separation. She is asking all of her inhabitants: "Have you treated me wrong, or have you treated me right?" "Will you continue to treat me wrong, or will you now begin to treat me right?"

"If you can not properly respect me, I must divorce you from my sphere of existence, because your foolish disrespect of me is killing me, as well as killing yourself."

"You have caused too much havoc and mischief in my atmosphere." "Either you get in harmony with me, or you get away from around me." She is not cruel. It is only self-defense. So, today she is cleansing her atmosphere with irregular rain, snow, hail, earthquakes, etc., seeking to restore her Ecological Balance, and her Environmental Peace. Okay...I still just want you to listen.

See, all of this is teaching us a very valuable lesson. We are not just discussing this to be discussing this. This is no vain and empty discourse. These facts are teaching us the Nature and the Science of the Current Time. So, pay close attention. Think in parallels. This is about you.

We have just learned that the Earth, is a prototype of the Mind and Womb. Right? Well, the Womb-Mind is the same thing as the Womb-Man, or Woman. Now, since this Earth is in perfected obedience to the will of God's plan, and she can not disobey, the nature and behavior of the Earth is clearly an instruction to us, as to what the proper nature and behavior of the Womb, the Mind, and the Woman should be, during these times. Our instructions are clear.

As the "Earth" is consciously dispelling the contaminants and contaminators from any interaction with herself, so should your "Mind" dispell it's contaminants, and those contaminators who seek to contaminate her purity and peace. Protect your Peace.

Now of course, as the "Earth" and "Mind" seek to purify themselves, so should the "Womb" or the "Woman", now cast the contaminants and the contaminators out from interaction with herself. This is done to protect the sanctity, purity, and peace of herself. She can not allow herself to be continually abused and spoiled, lest the fruit or children that she produces be also abused and spoiled. We are all those children from that Womb. You will hear this if you try.

The Virginous Womb, Mind, & Earth

The Womb-Mind and/or Woman must now, in this time, re-make herself into that original state of purity, peace, and virginity, that will allow her to give birth to the Children of Destiny...the Children of Divinity...the Children of God. Who else would a Goddess give birth to, other than the Children of God?

The Goddess Blackwoman is The Mother of Civilization, because she gives birth to "those children who will establish a state of civility on the planet", or throughout the world. Read that again please.

She co-creates Gods and Goddesses with The Divine Supreme Being, through the triple darkness of her womb. Yes, your entire being is made up from the substance of the "mineral matter in the Earth", the "chemical waters of the Womb", and the "electrical energies of the Mind"...up and out from triple darkness, three fertile wombs.

Body, Mind, Soul. These three wombs, in their virginous state, produce the Children of Destiny. The children of an elevated consciousness and purity of heart, that will rule the Earth with a Rod of Righteousness, a Rod of Freedom, a Rod of Justice, and a Rod of Equality. These are the children produced from "immaculate" conception. Clean Body of Vitality. Clean Mind of Thinking. Clean Heart of Intention. Immaculate.

It is only a "Virginous Woman" that can produce "Children of Destiny" or divine minds, as these we have described. The word "virginous" only means "pure". Just listen. The Earth maintains her "virginity" by only interacting or intercoursing with that seed which is "pure" and "virginous itself".

Just as the Earth, likewise, a "Goddess" maintains her "state of purity" by only allowing or entering into relations between herself and a "God" (meaning a Man in whom is the pure Living Spirit/Energy or Awakened Mental Consciousness of Divine).

When something pure enters into something else that is also pure, both things retain their "state of purity". No contaminants involved. Their virginity is not disturbed, allowing them to produce children of divine destiny, time and time again. And a "virgin" shall conceive. And a "pure woman" shall conceive.

Male/Female Relationship is The Foundation of Your Nation

Now, look, look, look. Why has all of this been said? Why has all of this been said? That is a lot to digest and understand even in it's simplicity, but still why has all of this been taught to us? Why? What is the Purpose?

This has been taught to us in order to inspire the thought of a new consciousness..a new style and fashion of thinking. This has been to inspire a new mind-state, or new approach, as to how we should deal with our present relationships, or the potential of any relationship that we might consider entering into.

This has been taught to inspire a new "sensitivity" and "awareness" to the importance of what you are doing. We now want to take our relationships **seriously**, now that we see how **seriously** our relationships take us...into good fortune or into bad fortune...Universal balance or imbalance...a state of order or a state a chaos. This is truly a matter of your own "life" or your own "death". You must deeply know this.

The healthy Male/Female Relationship is the supporting backbone of strength that is to uphold your entire Nation. Standing up on two legs, Blackman one leg, and Blackwoman the other.

The quality of your "Male/Female Relationship" directly determines the quality of the "Family" it produces. The quality of your "Family" directly determines the quality of the "Community" it produces. The quality of your "Community" directly determines the quality of the "Society" it produces. The quality of your "Society" directly determines the quality of the "Nation" it produces. And finally, the quality of your "Nation" directly determines the quality of the "World" it produces.

- Male + Female = **Family**
- Family + Family = **Community**
- Community + Community = **Society**
- Society + Society = **Nation**
- Nation + Nation = **World**
- World + World = **Universe**

This shows you how the condition of The Entire Universe can be adversely affected, or positively affected, simply from the rooted base of the male/female relationship. When a Man and Woman come together, they can literally "Move the World". Stop and think.

Now, listen, listen, listen. I hope that you

understand why all of this is being said to us. Have you been paying close attention? This is so very important. You, specifically, must drive this into your consciousness. You must get the point.

I want us to be clearly instructed on why it is so critically important for us to "consciously investigate", "consciously distinguish", "consciously discern", and "consciously discriminate" between those of whom we might contemplate entering into a relationship with.

See, no longer can we be unconsciously "careless" and unconsciously "irresponsible" in choosing the compatibility of our relationships, lest we be literally spoiled and soured into a state of miserable death, and stunted growth. We need to be happy ourselves, to produce happiness in our children. Plain and Simple. Simple and Plain.

And remember, these children produced, are all of us. These children are yourself projected into the future. You are currently preparing a Heaven or a Hell for these children, or your future self to live in. Enough about that.

The Earth, The Mind, The Womb has been carrying a weight that is not it's own...the weight of the contaminator and it's contaminants. The Earth, The Mind, The Womb, must cleanse, separate, and only accept that which is of it's own righteousness, that they may be free to be the purity of themselves. Save your life. It's the only way that you can save ours. Do...understand that. Please, do understand that.

Choosing The Proper Mate: The Absolute "Key" to a Successful Relationship!

Let us now examine the past and present mistakes in our relationships. Okay? So listen, how do you react and respond to men now? That is one of the original questions. What is going on in your present day relationships?

Are you still dating "black boys" today, because you can't seem to find any "Black Men"? Do you know what I mean? I mean, are you still dating "dead men" of whom you know ain't doing nothing in life, ain't going nowhere in life, and who ain't even thinking of doing nothing or going nowhere anytime soon in life?!!?

If you are still dating so-called men like these, why are you still doing so? Do you intend to marry a "dead man" like that? If not, then why are you wasting your time? What is your purpose?

If you have no reasonably-sane answer to that question, then you better shake the dust off of your shoes and start walking, before you end up dead too. *(Now of course, if you are already married to this dead man, I'm not trying to encourage you to just hastily divorce the poor fella. But in truth, many of you, who are married, are already divorced in mind and spirit anyway. That is the sad truth. We fall so quickly into divorce, because we so jump so quickly into marriage.)*

Blackwomen just can not continue to accept relations with dead Black Men, who refuse to grow past the immature state of "black boys". If you continue to grace him with the pleasure of your presence, he will think that it is okay to remain an immature child for the rest of his life. **You must now establish a required standard of quality, for the Man of whom you choose to relate to, because you have now established a required standard of quality for yourself.**

Think about it. If all Blackwomen today just absolutely refused to relate to any Blackman, who was being anything less than a True Blackman, you would be surprised at how much growth would all of a sudden take place! There would be True Blackmen everywhere! The woman doesn't realize the power of influence that she has. It is in her nature.

If you are serious about your relationships, then you will not date anyone of whom is less than the quality, or type of person, that you would consider marrying. For what other reason would you date a person, if they are not a potential candidate for marriage? You can have no other "sensible" reason. Don't continue to play the games and waste the time.

You should know by now that this is no game. And I know that you do not still intend to play the same little games as you used to play? Right? Right? Well, let us see. Answer these questions.

Do you still act "overly" submissive and weak, just to stroke the egos of men?...to get what you want? Remember that game? Do you? Are you being fake? Are you playing a role, just to maintain your relationship? Are you suppressing your own true character and potential so that you will not intimidate a man's insecure ego? Playing that "damsel in distress" role? Huh? Do you understand what I'm saying by "overly" submissive or "fake"? Do you understand the behavior that we are talking about?

This is what we're saying. I'm talking about that same type of "false character" and behavior that, we as Black people, have played in the presence of caucasian people. You know, that whole inferiority complex, denying who and what we truly are, just to make them feel comfortable and secure around us, or so that they would be our friends and associate with us. Yet caucasians bend not to comfort us.

Here we are bending over backwards to insure that they don't feel threatened by us, when they are the ones with the paranoidal fearful insecurity problem. Why should "we" stop being who and what God has blessed us to be, just because "they" are literally intoxicated with an emotional imbalance of insecurity?

Well listen, if it is wrong to compromise our natural behavior and character to make insecure caucasians feel less intimidated, should a woman act out this same false behavior to "pacify" and "perpetuate" the insecurities of a man?...of course not. No. If you "pacify" a person's insecurity, you "perpetuate" a person's insecurity.

Listen, if you are still doing this today in your relationships...then I ask you, why? Why are you being other than yourself? You are oppressing your own self. Be yourself. If a man is too weak to appreciate a strong, confident, Goddess of a Blackwoman, then is he really a man?! Or is he really still a little egotistical boy that still has some growing up to do?

Well, if he is still acting as a little boy, is he now ready and willing to grow-up? A strong Blackman wants a strong Blackwoman, because he knows that, one plus the other, equals a strong Black Nation. And he also knows that a strong Blackwoman makes him a strong Blackman.

So, if you are being "other than your true self" to maintain a relationship for whatever reasons, you have a little growing up to do as well, Blackwoman. Don't play games and don't play yourself. Don't disrespect yourself by settling for less than what you know is due to you, just because you want to be in a relationship. You will never ever be happy nor fulfilled, being untrue to your heart.
If you are "alone" and "lonely" right now, you will be just as "alone" and "lonely" in a so-called relationship, with someone of whom you know that you can not truly relate to. In fact, instead of being just "alone" and "lonely", you will be "alone", "lonely", and "miserable" too. Whatever you do, don't ever try to live a lie. You are now a Free Woman. Accept your own compatible mate, so that you may have the encouragement and opportunity to truly fulfill the total potential of yourself.

Are You Mentally Manipulating a Man?
You can not Live a Lie!

It seems that all of the games that we have played with our relationships, are centered around dishonesty or being untrue to others and ourselves. In our ignorance, this has caused many problems.

"Being ourselves" is a lesson that can not be stressed enough amongst Black people. We are forever trying to be something that we are not, but one would expect that type of behavior from a people who have lost their self-identity. And, as we can see, this illness creeps over into, and corrupts our relationships on every level.

Look at the falsehood that goes on in our so-called relationships today. Everyone is so un-authentic, playing some type of character role to manipulate people and situations, just to selfishly get what we want. It is insanity. It is insanity trying to live a lie.

Some of us disingenuinely manipulate our way into relationships by pretending to be something or someone that we are not, just to get a relationship...or just to be with somebody. But, why would you manipulate your way into a relationship, in which you know that you would not and could not be your true self?

Here you are presenting one character and personality of yourself to your friends, while you put up an entirely different, whole other character-role for your mate, so that you may manipulate him into being with you or staying with you, in that relationship. That is sad. That is absolutely sad.

Now, which one of these persons is the real you? And which one of these persons is it, that your poor deceived partner is in love with?...The "You #1" or The "You #2"? Are they in love with the "real you", or the other person that you pretend to be around them? Oh, this is a dangerous game that you play.

Don't you know that this is called "fraud"? Don't you know that this is called "deception"? Don't you know that this is just a "lie" incarnated, and animated through a person?...namely "you"? **People commit fraud through deception to get something that they would not get otherwise, if they were truthful.** Now, what is it that you are trying to get? What is it that you are trying to get by these unjust means?

Really now, just think about it. Is whatever you are getting in return, by mentally manipulating a person, worth living a lie and living as a liar for the rest of your entire life?...or even any part of your life? Are you so down and out desperate for a relationship, that you would lie, cheat, and manipulate just to get one? That is pretty bad. No, this is not so good. You need to stop and think. You need to stop and think about what you are doing, by seeking to deceive people. You really only deceive yourself. You hurt yourself.

What are you doing to yourself psychologically, spiritually, and emotionally? "Killing you". What are you doing to that man psychologically, spiritually, and emotionally? "Killing him". What are you doing to those children, who may be involved, psychologically, spiritually, and emotionally? "Killing them". You are killing everybody, including your own self! All of you will be mentally, therefore spiritually and emotionally wounded and scarred for life. Now, it just ain't worth all that, is it? No, it is not.

This one act of lying deception, out of this kind of selfish desperation, can hurt and hinder all other future relationships that you, he, the children and even your children's children may have.

If you build your house on a false foundation, it will all fall. If you build your family on a lie, it will all fall. Don't you ever try to live a lie. Never. You can never be successful. You will only deceive yourself, but you will hur us all! Do you understand?! Well, stop playing silly litt games! You are dealing with the Destiny of a Nation.

What is a "Relate" -tionship?

You want to build your family with a relations[illegible]p that is based upon a firm foundation of whol[illegible]some sincerity and rock-solid truth. And, in order to d[illegible]nis, you must have the proper building materials. N[illegible] just "any" materials, but the "proper" building materials.

Now, let me ask you a question. Is it so desperately important for you to have a relationship, that you would just be the companion of "any" Man? Come on? "Any Man?" Answer the question.

You can not have a "relationship" with just "any" man. Yes, you can "be together" with just any man, but that does not guarantee that you will have what is called a "relationship" with this person. Think about this thing.

Listen very closely. You can not be with just anybody to have what is called a "relationship", or rather a "fulfilling-relationship". You just can not do that.

Even though you may have seen men and women who, for many years, have been married and lived together all of their lives, that does not mean that they have had a "relationship" with one another. This is just the truth, and we have got to acknowledge it.

There are many people who are married today, but most of them have no "relationship" at all. Can you imagine being "married", to someone of whom you have no "relationship"? Can you imagine being "married", but left unhappy, dissatisfied, and unfulfilled? That is no "relationship" at all. Listen now.

A "relationship" is a "**relate**-tionship"...a "**relate**-tionship". Do you understand that? In order to have a "**relate**-tionship", two people must first be able to commonly "**relate**" to one another. Plain and simple. Okay? Do we get the point?

"**Relate**"-tionship. Think about it. "**Relate**"-tionship. Look at the word. "**Relate**"-tionship. Say the word with me, "**Relate**"-tionship.

This means "compatibility". The two persons must first be able to fluidly, harmoniously, reciprocally, and equitably share themselves with one another. Their similarities and differences must "compliment" and "balance" one another smoothly. And, it is this Basic Compatibility that fosters the basis for two Separate

Components to Naturally "**Relate**" to one another. Do you understand this clearly? I know that we all say we know this already, but we sure don't act like we know.

See, this understanding should obviously tell you that you can not just join together with just "anyone", and just expect to have a successful "**relate**-tionship"...although many of us foolishly try...although many of us foolishly try. I said, although many of us foolishly try, for various reasons of the same root of foolish insecurity. You better think about that one too.

Trying to build a Relationship on a "Fault-line"?

The ugly truth is that most of our relationships are not based on any "**Reciprocated Relations**" between two partners at all. No. Let's have the courage to be honest. In this day and in this time, we base our relationships on "Selfishly Vain Foundations".

Some are based on the insecurities and **fears of loneliness**, some are based on the insecurities of an **emotional dependency**, some are based on the insecurities and fear of losing a joined **financial security**, but very seldom are they based on an equally reciprocated "**relation of love**" one to the other. Do you hear me? You know that is the truth.

This is a horrifying truth, once you understand how this tragedy directly effects the world around you. If there is "war in the world", there is "war at home" between the male and female. If there is "peace in the world", there is "peace at home" between the male and female. But what is it that exists between the male and female today? War or Peace? Love or Tolerance?

You know that there is no actual "**relation of love**". "Love" itself is based on "agreement", and "agreement" is achieved on a "foundational point" or basis, upon which two or more different people can equally and mutually relate to one another harmoniously. Yet, of course love is not the basis of most relationships today.

Yes, yes, yes, and so our relationships fail one after the other...all because we attempted to build it on a weak, false, and invalid foundation. We attempt to build our relationships on top of a "fault-line"....a line of "fault" in our own life and insecure character. So, the relationship eventually falls. Obviously.

It was doomed to fall...it was doomed to fall from the very beginning. And it will be, and still is doomed to fall, everytime that we try to build-up a "relationship" on top of a foundation of "insecurity", "weakness", or "fault" in our own character...with someone of whom we know that we really can't "relate" to.

We always know deep in our hearts that we can't relate to the person, but we prolong the pain as we prolong the lie. "Honesty" can help us to avoid so much "Tragedy". **"Honesty" can help us to avoid so much "Tragedy".**

Yes, but wait a minute. Wait. Wait. We must say that, being true and honest, does not only mean making sure that the other person is compatible with you, but also making sure that "you" are compatible with that person. Yes, we must bring the balance.

If you seek a "Diamond of a Man", it is only fair that you make yourself a "Diamond of a Woman". Make sure that you truly "deserve what you desire", and that you truly "desire what you deserve". Be courageous enough to be honest. Hear that.

What is a "Fulfilling" Relationship?

It is only when two people are honestly, equally, and truly compatible for one another, that they can naturally provide a fulfilling reciprocating relationship for one another. There will be an equitable giving and receiving, back and forth. That is "<u>full</u>-filling relations" as opposed to "<u>half</u>-filling relations", where you have one person who is giving but not receiving, and one who is receiving and not giving.

This is really not a good thing, although so many of us dishonestly settle for this type of "half-filling" unequal so-called relationship. We have settled for this. We have just given-up. We really don't even believe in a "full-filling" relationship anymore. It is even hard for us to realistically imagine. So, we eventually settle for less than what we actually deserve because, deep in our hearts we believe that we actually deserve less.

Yes, it is always rooted right back into that low-self esteem and depth of self-hatred. Mental Slavery has inflicted a deep psychological trauma, that effects us in all aspects of life. Inferiority-Complex.

If there is not a back door to a building, we'll make one for ourselves. Inferiority-Complex. If there is not a back seat to a bus, we'll put one in for ourselves. Inferiority-Complex. If your man is "not" an abusive, low-life, no-good, game-playing fool, that breaks your heart every two weeks, then you will go find one who will break your heart! Right? Inferiority-Complex. You know who I'm talking to.

See, you really don't believe that you deserve anything better than the worst do you? Do you? We have become so accustomed to pain and unhappiness, that anything other than mistreatment doesn't even feel right to us. That is a shame. The truth must be told, admitted, accepted, and acknowledged.

It is this "Courage of Honesty" about our relationships, which will prevent all future chaos, and clear up all present chaos, that we may have gotten ourselves into, after building-up an imaginary relationship on the basis of falsehood. But, time erodes all falsehood, whereby it can no longer support it's own weight, let alone what we may have attempted to vainly build upon it. These old relationships must either be reproved or redefined right now, before the weight falls in on us all!

Yes, we all will feel the weight fall in on us! What if you get married? You then will have to spend the rest of your life trying to "pretend" that you are happy with this person that you settled for. This unhappiness will in turn affect every person in your home and every aspect of your family life. Your dissatisfaction and unhappiness will directly affect the life of your children. Your children will grow-up unhappy, and eventually become unhappy parents to their own children as well. And the cycle goes on and on.

See, if you are unfulfilled and empty inside, you will have nothing to give to your family. And you can not give what you do not have yourself. If you are not nurtured with the love that you need, you will not be able to properly nurture your family with the love that they need to grow, flourish, and be happy.

See, we need to understand how critically important choosing a mate is. **We must consider all of these things, before hand.** Choosing a mate can and will affect generations upon generations that are born from that one union. A Strong Family is built from a Strong Male/Female Relationship. And it is the weakened, Destroyed Family Life, that has caused so many of the Social ills that we endure today. Every person that is locked-up in a jail cell today, is being affected by some childhood scar of emotional pain, that they have rebelliously acted out in society.

Believe it or not, all of this pain and destruction can actually start from one bad decision to settle for a mate that is not really your spiritual-match or soul-mate. If there is no true harmony in your relationship, there will not be any true harmony in your family, and neither will there be harmony in their future families. Can you see this vicious cycle? A cycle that churns out dysfunctional human beings that are handicapped emotionally. Most of us have not beat this cycle.

So, sister please be patient, and do not disrespect

yourself by compromising your standards out of desperation. If you do, you will eventually be very sorry. And so will the rest of us.

Choose your mate very carefully. This is very important to the healthiness of your Nation. It is much easier said than done, but still it has to be done for the sake of yourself, your mate, your children, and your Nation.

•••

You and your mate should be created of a Single Essence. This brings Harmony, Balance, and Peace throughout cycles of times, generation upon generation.

Wisdom is given to you, so that you may avoid the pitfalls of destruction and despair. So, utilize that wisdom, in order to benefit from that wisdom. Don't suffer what you don't have to. Okay? Okay.

There is no need to be deeply unsatisfied and unfulfilled in the core of our own souls, in an attempt to live an impossibility...all because of dishonesty with our own selves.

Your nature yearns for a "full-filling relate-tionship". And there is no yearning in this Universe, that is meant to go unfulfilled. "Fulfilling Relate-tionships" can never be achieved with one of whom you can not compatibly "relate" to, but they can be achieved with one of whom you can. Be true. Be true. A "Fulfilling Relate-tionship is very possible, if you make it possible. Be patient. Be true...and you will have someone to love you for you.

Final Affirmation:

Your God created the Moon to relieve the Sun, the Day to enlighten the Night, the Water to cool the Fire, and the Heavens to amaze this Earth.

149

All things in this Universe were created with a complimentary balance...and surely there is one created for you. Be patient. Be true.

Character Reflection #12

"Fulfilling Relations" pt. 2

(constructive relations)

Okay, now we have to bring the balance. After receiving teachings, like some of these we have just received in Pt. 1 of this subject, we have to be very careful. If we are not careful, we could mess up the lives of ourselves and our families. Let me explain.

See, some of those teachings in Pt. 1, were primarily meant to boost the ego, of those specific women who suffer from inferiority or insecurity, so that their character may become more balanced. But if you are a woman, whose ego is imbalanced or largely inflated in the other direction, those teachings could make you more of the fool, than an inflated ego could already have you acting. Do you understand what I'm saying?

See, that is why we are not supposed to be taking someone else's medicine. Different medicines are prescribed for different people with different conditions. A normal sized ego is fine, but a "deflated ego", or an "inflated ego", will cause an imbalance in the character of the individual. So, you need a different prescription to achieve "your" balance.

Yes sister, I'm talking to you right there, with the inflated ego imbalance. "You". Yes, we are getting ready to talk to you. You know you need some talking to. Don't you? Yes, you do. Yes, we need to talk to you before you end up destroying the relationship that you already have. Yes, let's talk.

Are You At War With Man?

Now, I just know that you got fired up, after reading some of that other teaching in Pt. 1 of this subject. You know, the teaching about not putting up with "black boys", who refuse to be Men, and about not suppressing your own strength to pad the insecure egos of Men. Remember that? You liked that part, didn't you? Yes, you did. I could hear you thinking, as you were reading. You just loved that part!

You were saying, ***"That's right! That's right! If a Man is too weak to handle a strong Blackwoman, then he must not be a Man!!!" If he is too weak to accept me as myself, then he just better find him somebody else!!!"***

"I'm The Mother of Civilization up in here, and I'm running things today, so get out of my way!!!" "Ain't no Man gonna keep me from being myself!!!" "I'm The Blackwoman!!!"

Ohhhh...just sit on down somewhere with all of that. All that huffin and puffin and carrying-on. What you talking about? You ain't no Blackwoman without no Blackman, so just sit all of that on down. You know you just crazy, making all of that noise. Now, we have to stick a pin in your inflated ego too. Your ego is almost as bad as a Man's.

Yes, before you get too excited and lose your thinking, let's bring the balance to this subject. Yes, let's bring the balance.

Listen now. Yes, it is very true that you should be "strong" and have the courage to "be yourself" in the face of any man and anybody, but how can you "be" that which you don't properly know nor understand? Do you even "know yourself", enough to "be yourself"?

See, I don't want you to naively take these teachings out of context, and run off to make a mess of your life and relationships, trying to be "Miss Macho-Woman", running up to combat a man every chance that you get. No, that is just the sickness of insecurity in another form.

To stand-up and "be yourself", does not mean to stand-up by stepping-down on a man. You are not to go to war with your Man. No. You do not manifest your own strength by attempting to tear down another's strength. No, let's bring the balance.

You need to stand-up in Divine Strength as a Goddess Blackwoman, but a Goddess Blackwoman is not a foolish Blackwoman. She is wise. She is artful. She is civilized, and she knows The Arena of Her Own Strength. Think about what is being said to you.

Define, Determine, and Develop Your own Feminine Strength

Understand that you are to manifest the strength of your own individual Feminine Nature, that the Universe has created within "You". It is all too often that women have misunderstood, and thought that to exert a Strength of Character, meant to exert a Masculine Character. But, this is clearly a misunderstanding.

The Liberation of Women is not about being liberated to run up behind a Man trying to imitate him. Your liberation is about having the freedom to express the Divine Genius that Your God has put in you! Your liberation comes from having the freedom to express that Divine Genius, through your Own Medium and Expression of Strength.

No, the Man is not the yardstick by which you are to measure "Your" strength. You can not accurately measure the strength of a "Woman", in comparison to a "Man". No, you just don't do that, because you are dealing with two totally different components. We can not say that a Woman is not strong, based upon the observation that she is not exerting her strengths as a Man would exert his. That is improper.

That is like measuring the Sun by the Earth, or the Earth by the Sun. It would be foolish to say that "The Sun" is inadequate, because it does not produce vegetation, or other animated life forms on it's surface like "The Earth" does. Just as it would also be foolish to say that "The Earth" is inadequate, because it does not produce inflamed gases that belch-out from it's surface, projecting light and heat as "The Sun" does. You do not compare them one to the other to determine their function and duty, or to measure their worth and value. You just don't do that.

The Sun and The Earth are two totally different Types of Planets that work together harmoniously to produce life as we know it. They are both Planets, but they express and exert their own individual Strengths of Character, through their own Universal Purpose and Nature. The Sun was created to have it's function, and The Earth was created to have it's function. And they work together.

Well listen now, these signs in The Universe are for you and I to learn from. No more should you attempt to measure your strength of femininity by the standards of masculinity. Do you think that Masculinity has a monopoly on strength or something? Blackwoman, Define, Determine, Develop, and Be the strength of your own Self-Identity. Your Brother, has a totally different function of nature. You stand up on your own Universal Foundation, Purpose and Principles. You are a Wonder-filled Blackwoman! Just take the time to dig within to discover those innate Wonders!

Now, listen closely. I hope that you will pay attention to these things. Some sisters may understand these things more than others, but still everyone should listen. There are Keys all throughout these writings, for those who would seek them out, dig them out, and think them out. These writings are pregnant, to those who can unearth the rest of the riches. So, let's just listen.

The Feminine Power is the Great Power of "Rebirth" and/or "Nurturance". The act of **"Nurturance"** is a skill and an artform, that requires the unified ingredients of **"Intelligent Wisdom"** combined with an **"Enduring Love"**. This nurturing mixture is needed, in order to effectively and skillfully evolve life from one stage of developing maturity to the next.

"Nurturance" is a skill and an artform. And if you want to see The Master of this Skillful Art, you just study the methodology of God Allah. I don't think you really have heard what was just said, but we will have to talk about all of that in another forum.

Don't Nag him to Death!
Nurture him to Life!

But listen...the original, original, original point that we want to focus on, is this. If you see that there is an insecurity, a character flaw, or an ego problem with a brother, you do not want him to continue living in that error. But, you don't want to go to war with him either. Right? Right. Okay.

As we said earlier, you just can not simply say "***...If a Man is too weak to handle a strong Blackwoman, then he must not be a Man!!!" If he is too weak to accept me as myself, then he just better find him somebody else!!!"***

Don't go busting-up your relationships trying to be that Miss-Macho Woman...going to war with your mate. A relationship is for "Constructive" means, not "Destructive" means. That is not the way.

So, the question is, "what is the way?" How will you attempt to correct the weaknesses that you may see in him?

(The answer really is simply: Do unto others as you would have them do unto you.) But, what will you do, to try and get him to change his behavior and/or character? The better question is: What "should" you do?

Well, you might come to understand what it is that you "should do", once you understand what you "should not do". And, the first thing that you do not want to do, is to "nag him", "drag him", and "beat him down" with the power of your mouth. You do not want to go to war with a Man. That is not wise, for many reasons.

But, we have to talk about this, because there are so many sisters at war with their own Blackmen! I absolutely do want to encourage you to be a strong Blackwoman in all situations...but when it comes to your relationships, I don't want you to think that, to exert the strength of your "Womanhood" is to tear down the strength of his "Manhood"! No, that is incorrect! That is incorrect! That is incorrect! You are to uplift your Blackman!!! Not contest Him!!!

You sisters, who think and act like you are at war with the Man, I want you to listen real good. You know that the society, in which we live, works to aggressively tear down and destroy Your Blackman on a constant everyday basis, and now "you" want to join the Wrecking Crew too??? Oh no, that is absolutely wrong! That is your own insanity!

You know good and well, that The Whole World is beating up on his Manhood all day long, and as soon as he gets home, here you are swinging at him too!!! What's wrong with you? Have you lost your mind? Yes, of course you have, because after you just completely destroy what is left of him, what do you have left to love? What do you have left that you can respect? Nothing. Nothing at all.

He will never be strong enough to uplift you as a Woman, if you are constantly tearing down his "Manhood". He will never have the inclination to love you if are constantly contesting him!!! A relationship is no

"Contest"! It is a "Unified-Partnership"! You are on the same side! Uplift him and he will Uplift you. Uplift his Manhood, and his Manhood will uplift your Womanhood. That is the balance.

Now, I hope that you know which sisters, that this message is for. This is "your" medicine to bring you a balance. Because, as we said in pt. 1, to uplift him does not mean to continue to passively sit back doing nothing, as some women have done, by allowing an insecure man's "false" ego to get out of hand. No. That is not building him, that is de-constructing him.

You do not want your companion standing up on the imagined strength of a false foundation, you want to nurture and encourage him to stand up on the firm foundation of "truth" and of "true confidence". If you allow him to be built up on the foundation of anything other than the truthful concrete reality of himself, you are just setting him up, higher and higher, for an inevitable great fall. You have got to be true to yourself and to him.

I'm serious, you really do not want to continue feeding into that type of behavior, by continuing to prop up that little fragile "false" ego. You would just be creating a monster that will eventually come back to haunt you. You will end up having a Real Big Fool around the house, if you don't deal straight up with that "false" ego.

The point is, to be straight-forward and honest when dealing with him, but you don't have to be a "terrorist" when dealing with him, trying to attack the brother. It is all about balance. See, it is in situations as this, where you want to employ The Strength of Your Universal Nature. This is when you want to wisely apply the constructive skill of "Nuturance", to effectively and skillfully evolve or "nurture" his mind-state and his thinking from one stage of developing maturity to the next. Only then, can you both grow on in peace.

The Blackman's Ego should be Handled With Care

Egos are a "fragile thing". And "fragile things" are those that you want to "handle with care". Hear this now. You do not want to decimate and destroy the ego of your Man, because, in truth, that is what you love about him. Yes, you do.

But, when an "ego" is misguided and uncontrolled, it can be destructive to it's atmosphere. Yet, at the same time, an "ego" which is guided aright and well disciplined, can become the most powerfully creative force that you ever want to see.

Yes, I know that your Blackman broods a lot of "ego" today, but it is "false ego". It is actually insecurity masquerading as the power of "ego". But, as your man, you want him to be filled with real or authentic "ego", "strength", and "power". That is the only way that you are going to truly respect him. And you want to respect him. Yes, you do.

See, you actually want to encourage his "true ego", because you should understand that his "true ego" is actually his "will power". And when his "will power" becomes directed by the Intelligence of The God, and disciplined by the righteous Character of The God, he will actually become a manifestation of "The Will of The God"! He will actually become a "Real Man"! He will Man-ifest! The Living Goddess will finally have a Living God by her side! A Living Real Man! And it is a "Real Man" that you have been looking for all the days of your life. Oh, you know it's true. Yes, you do.

Use Your Powers For Good!

Now look, I really didn't want to go too deeply off into all of that, but I just wanted to make a simple point. You are a mighty powerful Blackwoman, whether you know it or not. You just need to learn how to use your powers for good. Yes, for good.

The Supreme God did not create your feminine powers, for you to use them in warfare against the masculine powers of a man. Your powers were created to compliment the masculine, as are the masculine meant to compliment the feminine. Use your powers to console, comfort, compliment, and balance Your Blackman, as you should seek the same from him. We want Constructive Relations, not the Destructive Relations that we have been so familiar with in the past.

You are the prototype of Mother Earth, and her powers are invested in you. Look at you. You are made into the most "attractive" being on the planet! The Essence fo Beauty Itself. It is true. Look at your power. You can just stand still, look beautiful, and actually change the thought, direction, and course of any Man that tries to walk by you! That is power. That is true "Man-ipulation". You can move and attract men to you with hardly any effort at all.

Well, seriously, this "attraction" power is just another word for "gravity"...or the "power of pull". You have this power, and The Earth has this power of gravitational pull. The Earth naturally attracts or magnetically pulls all objects, within its atmosphere, right back down to its surface. But, you are different in that, you can control the direction of your "gravity", or your "power of pull". You can pull your atmosphere up, or you can pull it down. You already do this unconsciously, depending upon your mood. Yes, you do.

Look, all of this is being said to say that, your "power of pull" is what fuels your "Power of Nurturance". To "nurture" something, is to "pull" something up into it's different stages of developing potential. This "pulling power" is one of the key strengths of your nature.

Well, look now. Your Blackman has been knocked down by The World, and broken into pieces. Now, who in This World is going to pick him up and put him back together again? Better yet, who has the power to put him back together again? You do!

You are the prototype of The Womb itself, so you can rebirth anything with just the power of your Nurturing Nature! Yes, you can do this once you return to your Original Mind State! It is absolutely true! And those who have destroyed your Blackman know this to be true, and fear this truth about you and your potential!!! Yes they do!

This is why they want to do everything within their persuasive power, to keep you **dissatisfied with** Your Blackman, **upset with** Your Blackman, **at war with** Your Blackman, and **divided from** Your Blackman, so that you will never even think to have enough "love" for him, to "nurture his insecurities", "heal his wounds", or put him back together again!!!! Divide and Conquer!!! Do you hear me???? You had better listen!!!

You are the only Woman in this World, that does not have a Man!!! Your Man has been taken away from You!!! Your Man has been attacked and Murdered!!! His Mind is Dead! His Character is Dead! His Will is Dead!

He was and is systematically broken down and destroyed by your historical enemy. And then your enemy hides his guilty hands, turns to the Blackwoman, and has the nerve to say, "See, I told you he was no good. He is no Man at all. You have no hope in him, so come on and join me." Can you believe that! He kills your Man, and blames him for being dead.

So, now what are you going to do??? You have no Companion! You have nothing and no one left to love, nor do you have anyone to love you! You have been made a into a Widow!!! Do you understand me??? Now, what are you going to do about it???

You Mad and Upset, because your Blackman is Dead, and all that you can do is sit there beating and cursing The Corpse??? What in the hell is that supposed to do??? You had better act like you got some sense, and start doing some life saving techniques, lest you and your daughters be widows for the rest of your lives! That is "Your" Man dying!

"Your Man"! "Your" Man! "Yours"!

You had better learn how to use that power of gravity, to pull the scattered pieces of that Blackman back together again! And, once you do that, you had better use your "Power of Nurturance" to breathe life back into him again. Sometimes all it takes is a little Love and Understanding. I said "Love and Understanding", not "Cursing and Contesting". "Love and Understanding", not "Dragging and Nagging". "Love and Understanding" You have to learn how to "wisely" apply the Powers of Your Nature.

It is interesting, that you are in the same position as The Great Queens of Africa, when the barbarian invaders from the North had finally killed off all of their Black Men in battle after battle after battle. All of their Men were dead! So, these Warrior Queens stood up and went to battle with these barbarian enemies until they could nurture their own male children into Warriors for their Nation again! They no longer had Men for themselves, but they were determined to make sure that their daughters would have men for the next generation, and Warrior Men at that!!! That is the right spirit!

Now, here you are today, your Man is dead, and people making warfare against you everyday, but you still don't realize that you are in a state of war. I guess you think that your Blackman is dying from natural causes? You better wake up! These Great Warrior Queens are sending you a message to the future of what you must do today, in this modern-day "Mental Warfare"!

Know the time and what must be done! You have to "Rebuild and Rebirth" Your Blackman! He is all that you have! You know that he has been knocked in the head, and therefore don't have too much good sense left! But, what are you going to do? Heal his wounds, or further inflict wounds on his dead body? You two are "family"! Don't go to war with him! Don't play into the hands of your enemy!

Everywhere he goes, somebody is trying to rub salt

in his wounds! You are his only chance for survival! You are his only chance to be healed! And what I am trying to tell you is that you are "A Healer" by nature! Heal that Man! He is all that you have, and you are all that he has!

See, and when a Man recognizes a Woman that is "down with him", a Woman that "has his back", a Woman that is willing to "be his Refuge of Rebirth and Regeneration", that Man will move Heaven and Earth to please, protect, provide for, and uplift that Woman of whom his Soul Delights!!! Oh, yes he will! And that is the kind of Man that your nature yearns for. Yes, it does.

You don't have to be a Widow forever, if you learn how to use your own feminine power "constructively". You were created with the attractive gravitational powers to pull him wherever you want to pull him, so pull him up! PULL HIM UP!!!! Use your powers to re-make and re-birth Your Blackman!

Although, just remember one thing. This is key. You can only heal a Man, that "wants" to be healed. Find that Man who is seeking Life, as you are seeking Life. A Goddess can only help those, who "want to help themselves". Remember that. Remember that. Remember that. That is law. If you remember that, it will save you a lot of pain, strain, and time. You can only re-birth a man, who sincerely wants to get up and live.

•••••

Now, we have spent quite some time talking about this subject of "Fulfilling Relations" and "Constructive Relations". And, a "Fulfilling Relationship" can only be "fulfilling", if it is constantly "constructing" a sense of "fulfillment" in both persons involved.

But still, why have we spent so much time and energy on this subject matter? This is because your interpersonal relationship with a male plays such a vital role to your development as a Goddess Blackwoman. A

Goddess is the embodiment of Peace itself, of Paradise itself, of Heaven itself. And it is your responsibility to reproduce or multiply this peace all around the world. The Mother of Peace.

Yet, in order to "give this peace" you must first "achieve this peace" for yourself. And, your wise brother, The Honorable Elijah Muhammad, has taught that "*When two people are together and are at peace, they are in Heaven. What is above the peace of Husband and Wife?*"

This automatically teaches us that the Woman is the Heaven of Man, and the Man is the Heaven of Woman. But if you are not with the proper Man, or he is not with the proper Woman, they can be other than Heaven to each other...quite the opposite actually.

The proper Woman, is a Woman in submission to the will, duties, and character of The God. The proper Man, is a Man is submission to the will, duties, and character of The God. A Goddess and a God standing up together, living to project the light and love of The Most Supreme God. It can be achieved. It must be achieved. It shall be achieved.

Final Affirmation:

"What is The Man without His Woman, and what is The Woman without Her Man?"

"Such is the incompletion, of the Single Essence of God." One Love.

Concluding thoughts on:
Character Cleansing
(Examine & Cleanse)

In closing...I would like to say, that I personally, am not a Master of these teachings, yet these teachings I strive to Master. And, it is a requirement that we all make an honest effort to constantly incorporate the blessings of a righteous and peaceful mind-state, into all areas of our lives. This is the only way to maintain and achieve peace, by allowing the best principles in us to take root and then grow up into every aspect of our lives. Then, The Success of Peace, grows beyond a "Mind-state" into a full grown "Life-state". That is the Destined Goal.

This is a walk forward on the constant path of purification or healing. So, let this Character Cleansing portion of this book, serve as a constant Self-examination, like a daily check-up with the Doctor. Review it regularly.

Living within this society, we have been infected with so many mental impurities, and inflicted with so many emotional injuries, that we now desperately seek to be healed. God Allah is taking us through a "re-constructive surgery". But, in order to be "admitted-patients" of The Doctor, we must at least have the courage enough to "admit" that we are sick, and in need of healing. Then we must willingly submit to the Doctor by lying still on the operating table...pain and all. Do you know what I mean?

It is only through a thorough, and an honest Self-Examination, that our imbalances are revealed to us. So constantly Self-Examine. Examine the content of your character in private? Examine the content of your character in public? Is it different, or the same? Is it righteous or is it mischievous?

Examine the motives in your heart for doing the things that you do. Are your motives pure, or are they less than pure? For what root reason do you do what you do? Examine, and cleanse. Examine, and cleanse. Examine, and cleanse.

Examine and analyze everything within the sphere of your entire life. The more we improve the quality of our personal selves, the more we improve the quality of our lives, and the lives of those around us. That's the mission. Examine and Cleanse.

Final Affirmation:

We must at least have the will, to sincerely "attempt" to perfect all that we perceive to be imperfect. That is God's will.

You have a divine responsibility...for "No Nation can rise higher than it's Woman". So Rise Blackwoman...Rise.

12 Point Review

REFLECTION #1

"Attitude/Character Projection"

A"God-Essence-Blackwoman" projects the Peace, Power, and Presence of Divinity in Person.

Carry The Atmosphere of God wherever you go, and it will carry you also."

REFLECTION #2

"Maturity"

When I was a child, I thought, acted, and understood as a child. But now, as a Queen Mother of Civilization, I must do away with childish things.

I must become an example to the child, that the child may be guided aright.

REFLECTION #3

"Peer-Pressure/Self-Validation"

Does it profit us to seek the "praise" of fools, or to seek the "respect" of God Allah, whom is The Eternally Wise?

Treasure your own Self-respect...it's the pillar of your strength.

REFLECTION #4

"Idle-Chatter"

If you are not saying anything, please do not say anything. Thank You.

REFLECTION #5

"Emotional Thinking"

Whosoever controls your emotions, is thereby in control of you.

Yet, if you control your own emotions, you will thereby have Self-control.

REFLECTION # 6

"Posture of Pride"

Even though a Goddess walks with her head up high, she makes certain that her feet never steps on anyone down low.

Even though her back stands firm and tall, she keeps it flexible enough to bend-over and lift-up the down-fallen sister or brother.

...for a Goddess understands that the only thing in between high and low, is the merciful Grace of God Allah.

REFLECTION #7

"Indecent Exposure"

The Radiance of your True Beauty begins within your "heart and mind".

Strive to Beautify your inner-self, then watch it's glow radiate to the surface of your physical, and beyond.

Yes, and just as surely as you allow this Beauty to emanate out from you, it shall surely return unto you. Goddesses attract Gods. And Queens attract Kings.

REFLECTION #8

"Grooming Habits"

"You will only feel as good as you look, and you will only look as good as you feel!"

"Self-Image is a Master-Key towards Self-Love."

REFLECTION #9

"Orderliness"

God's mission is to resurrect the life out of death, and to spark the light out of darkness, which is to bring the Order out of Chaos.

The Peace is where you bring it, and The Heaven is where you make it. So, be...and it is.

REFLECTION #10

"Effective Communication"

"Speak the uplifted Words of The God", in sincerity...and you will eventually "Become the uplifted Words of The God", in sincerity.

"...And The Word became Flesh."

REFLECTION #11

"Productive Living"

God created "all" living things on purpose, including you.

Are you "living" on the purpose for which you were created? Invest your time productively.

REFLECTION #12

"Fulfilling Relations Pt. 1"

Your God created the Moon to relieve the Sun, the Day to enlighten the Night, the Water to cool the Fire, and the Heavens to amaze this Earth.

All things in this Universe were created with a complimentary balance...and surely there is one created for you. Be patient. Be True.

"Fulfilling Relations Pt. 2" (constructive relations)

"What is The Man without His Woman, and what is The Woman without Her Man?"

"Such is the incompletion, of the Single Essence of God." One Love.

FINAL WORD

"Be Yourself"

(Concluding Thoughts on Divine Responsibility)

Now, I want you and I to understand the importance and value of the whole of this lesson. The whole message is about "being yourself". And what is yourself???...a Righteous Goddess.

This is a responsibility dear sister. And, in order to be effective, in your responsibility, your character and image must be the truth! I can not stress honesty enough...honesty to self and honesty to others.

As we all seek to take on these few principles of righteous character, we must be sincere to the core. We must truly be ourselves. It really takes courage to do that. These few principles are not presented to you that you may simply act them out blindly. No. You do not want to be an outer "symbol" of righteousness with no actual inner "substance" of righteousness. No, we just don't need that.

Whatever you do, don't be fake. You can only fool yourself. If these principles are not yet you, be yourself while you patiently strive to make these principles a living reality in your life. You are to submitting your "past slave-character", to become the character of a Proud Goddess Blackwoman, which is truly yourself. These are principles to "practice", not principles to "pretend". Only sincerity will bring you success. Be the truth.

Our responsibility is in the service to our people. And they can sense fakeness a mile away. The only way to foster a "sincere" change in them, is to respect them by being totally "sincere". Only then will your efforts be effective. Your heart must be true.

• • •

Your "best" you is coming to birth. Your "Goddess" you is coming to birth. And, coming to birth is a process that demands time and therefore perseverance. And remember that the higher you aim in your striving, the higher you will hit in your achievement.

I also want you to fully understand the purpose for projecting your righteous image and character in the midst of your people. Your projected image is supposed to make a revolutionary, evolutionary, psychological, effect upon those who have gone contrary to the way of righteousness, but most importantly it will also reinforce the righteousness that is within yourself!!! (Self-image, Self-esteem, Self-love)

Your positive character of personality must be strong enough to "out-magnetize" the current negative social forces that attract and grip our people. And we shouldn't be afraid to study the intelligent genius in the methodology of those negative forces. We study this science that we may take those same laws of magnetic attraction, and switch the polarity to a positive means. A Master martial artist doesn't directly resist the blow of an opponent, the master just redirects the energy of the blow back onto the opponent.

Our magnetism must be stronger than the opponent! Our marketing, promotion, and advertising of Righteousness, must be stronger and wiser than the marketing, promotion, and advertising of Filth, Wickedness, and Indecency! We are marketing, promoting, and advertising the benefits of Righteous Living! Civilized Living.

We seek to persuade our people to make an investment in the best of themselves, that in turn they may receive the riches of life, and receive it more abundantly. So make sure that you are constantly cultivating your own investment, that they may see your success, and know why you are succeeding.

Magnetize your people. Everything from your verbal language to your body language, from your outer image to the inner image of your character, should be calling and attracting your people towards righteousness. Your very lifestyle and your total being will be a **"Calling to the Faith"**. As a Goddess Blackwoman, you are "The Caller to The Faith"...calling your people home, who have gone astray.

And so now, I'm calling you...all of you who would have the courage to "accept what is your own, and be what is yourself". We have business to handle. The resurrection of The Gods and The Goddesses...The Blackman and Blackwoman. This is a call To The Creams of The Planet. The cream always rises to the top.

I hope that you have enjoyed the reading. Thank you for your time, attention, and patience. Love' y'all. Peace.

Final Affirmation:

Remember: "Peace given, is surely Peace returned".

Goddess Blackwoman

Contractual Agreement

• • • • • • • • •

On this brand-new day of (date)____________, I, (your name)______________________ do hereby declare myself to be a **"Righteous Goddess Blackwoman"**.

This means, that I agreeably commit to consistently and persistently, work, strive, and struggle towards making me the best me that I can possibly be.

My root objective and goal, is to establish Peace and Righteousness in this Universe, yet I understand that this first begins by establishing Peace and Righteousness within Me.

In this mission, I am accepting my own responsibilities, as **"The Mother of Civilization"**, and being my own true self, as a **"Righteous Goddess Blackwoman"**. My word is my bond. And my bond is with God. Now and Forever.

Parties in Agreement:

Signed: __________________________(your name)

Date: ___________________

Signed: __________________________(your name)

Date: ___________________

(**By signing, I verify that the above pledge is true, factual, and sincere to my heart. I have accepted my own, to become myself. None shall turn me away from being a "Righteous Goddess Blackwoman" again.)

Dedication To The Blackwoman

Black eyes, Black mind, Black spirit, and Black soul
Blackwoman, my heart you shall forever own.
The depth of your darkness is divine to behold
Never behind me, but always beside me,
through it all.

Never will I dishonor you or dethrone you as my queen,
without you I am incomplete, as nothing.

That day will come again
when the whole world will know you as I do
The womb of life, the mother and giver of all that is good,
and all that is true.

You are my Divine Black Goddess alone
Now and forever, I celebrate you, I honor you, I respect you,
and I love you as you are Blackwoman
For without your hand, I would be less than a true Blackman.

Akil '91 ©

A Brief Listing of Relevant
Reading & Listening Sources

In The Spirit
Susan Taylor

Blackwomen of Antiquity
Ivan Van Sertima

Acts of Faith
Iyanla Van Zant

Tapping The Power Within
Iyanla Van Zant

In The Company of My Sisters
Julia A. Boyd

Good Hair for Colored Girls
Lonnice Bonner

When Beauty Touches Me
Cornrows & Co.

Women and their Fathers
Victoria Secunda

Return to The African Mother Principles of Male and Female Equality (Volume I)
Oba T'Shaka

Self-Love/Developing and Maintaining Self-Esteem
Rosenna Bakari

Lectures: * (312) 602-1230 to order
How To Give Birth To A God (pt. 1 - pt. 5)
Min. Louis Farrakhan Chicago 1987

The Great Power & Value of Blackwomen
Min. Louis Farrakhan San Diego 1990

A Nation Can Rise No Higher Than It's Woman
Min. Louis Farrakhan Atlanta 1994

Respect For Womanhood: Acquiring The Mind of God
Min. Louis Farrakhan Chicago 1987

The Blackwoman at War
Sis. Min. Atty. Ava Muhammad Philadelphia 1994

Principles of Femininity Pt. 1 & 2
Sis. Min. Atty. Ava Muhammad 1991 & 1993

OTHER BOOKS BY AUTHOR

1. **From Niggas To Gods Pt. 1**
   Akil (250 pgs. Nia Comm./Press $11.95)

2. **Religious Confusion vs. The Black Spiritual Rise**
   Akil (80 pgs. Nia Comm./Press $7.95)

PARTIAL LISTING OF BLACK BOOKSTORES NATIONALLY

ALABAMA

*AFRIKA NOW, 2032 AIRPORT BLVD., MOBILE, AL 36606...(205) 476-7040,

*CRESCENT IMPORTS, 1001 N. MEMORIAL PKWY, HUNTSVILLE, AL 35810...(205) 851-6566

*WISDOM HOUSE, 2022 DARTMOUTH AVE., BESAMER AL 35020...(205) 424-0170

ARKANSAS

*GENESIS BOOKSTORE,1722 S. UNIVERSITY AVE., LITTLE ROCK, AK 72204...(501) 664-8142

*IMAGES OF AFRICA, 1236 S. MAIN, LITTLE ROCK AK 72202...

*NUBIAN BOOKS, 4405 W. 12TH ST., LITTLE ROCK AK 72204...

*PYRAMID GALLERY & BOOKS, 1308 S. MAIN, LITTLE ROCK AK 72202...(501) 372-5824

*ZAWADI COLLECTIONS, 924 S. OAK ST., LITTLE ROCK, AK 77204...(501) 664-2665,

CALIFORNIA

*ALI'S AFROCENTRIC, 2164 S. POPPY, FRESNO, CA 93706...(209) 445-3130

*CAROL'S BOOKS, 5679 FREEPORT BLVD., SACREMENTO, CA 95822...(916) 428-5611

*(THE) CONNECTION, 6183 IMPERIAL AVE., SAN DIEGO, CA 92114...(707) 427-3438

*CULTURE CONNECTION, 1010-B FLOKIN #2225, SACREMENTO, CA 95831...(916) 427-7715

*ESO WON BOOKS, 900 N. LA BREA BLVD., INGLEWOOD, CA 90302...(310) 674-6566,

*GRASSROOTS BOOKS, 4441-43 W. SLAUSON AVE., LOS ANGELES, CA 90043...(213) 296-1997

*IT IS WRITTEN, 6934 FEDERAL BLVD., LEMON GROVE, CA 91945...(619) 677-4173

*MALIQ'S BOOK PALACE, 4058 CRENSHAW BLVD., LOS ANGELES, CA 90008...(213) 294-1311

*MARCUS BOOK STORES, 3900 MLK WAY, OAKLAND, CA 94609... (510) 652-2344,

*MARCUS BOOK STORES, 1712 FILMORE ST.,SAN FRANCISCO, CA 94115... (415) 346-4222

*OAKLAND KEMETIC, 5755 MARKET ST. #1, OAKLAND CA 94608... (510) 601-0400

*PHOENIX INFO CTR, 115 E. RIALTO AVE, RIALTO CA 92376... (909) 820-1264

*PYRAMID BOOKS, 5911 UNIVERSITY AVE. #317, SAN DIEGO, CA 92115...

*THE BLACK CLOTH HANGER, 503 MARINA CENTER, SUISON, CA 94585...(707) 427-3438

*UNITY TIMES BOOKS & TAPES, 15429 GEMSTONE CT., MARENO VALLEY, CA 92553...(909) 485-1626

COLORADO

*HUE-MAN EXPERIENCE BOOKSTORE, 911 PARK AVENUE WEST, DENVER,CO 80205... (800) 346-4036,

*THE BLACK MARKET, 2547 WELTON, DENVER, CO 80205...(303) 298-8922

*THE TATTERED COVER, 1536 WYNKOP, DENVER, CO 80202...(303) 322-7727

*THE UNDERGROUND RAILROAD BOOKSTORE, 4878 CHAMBERS RD., DENVER, CO 30236...(303) 373-2903

CONNECTICUT

* BLACK PRINT HERITAGE GALLERIES, 162 EDGEWOOD AVE., NEW HAVEN, CT 06511

*BROTHERS, 445 ALBANY AVE., HARTFORD, CT 06120... (203) 247-0663

*UBTSI ART STUDIO, 61 ROSE ST., DANBURY, CT 06810...

DELEWARE

*HANEEF BOOKSTORE, 911 ORANGE ST., WILMINGTON, DE 19801...(302) 656-4193,

FLORIDA

*AFRO-IN BOOKS & THINGS, 5575 NW 7TH AVE., MIAMI, FL 33127...(305) 756-6107,

*BOOKS A MILLION #312, 90 NORTH NOVA RD., DAYTONA, FL 32114...(904) 255-5588

*ENA ENTERPRISES, 17583 CARVER AVE., JUPITER, FL 33458...(407) 743-4240

*ESSENCE BOOKSTORE, 16929 S.W. 103RD AVE., ARCHER, FL 32618...(904) 495-9523

*FLORIDA A&M BOOKS, UNION BUILDING, TALLAHASSEE, FL 32307...(904) 599-3070

*FUTURE VISION,1105 34TH ST. SOUTH, ST. PETERSBERG, FL 33711...(813) 321-2203

*O.B. BOOKSTORE, 1447 MYRTLE AVE., JACKSONVILLE, FL 32209...

*OMNI BOOKS, 99 S.W. 34TH ST. GAINESVILLE, FL 32607...(904) 375-3755

*ZAWADI OJA AFRIKA, 1409 SOUTH MAIN ST., GAINESVILLE, FL 32601...(904) 491-7365

GEORGIA

*AFRICAN HERITAGE BOOKS, 503 EAST ANN ST., VALDOSTA, GA 31601...

*1ST WORLD BOOKSTORE, 86 UPPER ALABAMA ST. ATLANTA, GA 30303...(404) 681-2042,

*CRESCENT STAR, 617 LIVINGSTON ST.,SYLVESTER, GA 51791...(912) 890-7963

*COBBS BOOKS, 511 A. S. SLAPPY BLVD., ALBANY, GA 31701...(912) 454-0400

*MEDU BOOKSTORE, 2841 GREENBRAIR PKWY, ATLANTA,GA 30331...(404) 346-3263,

*OMAR'S BOOKSHOP, 144 N. WAYNE ST., MILLEDGEVILLE, GA 31061...(912) 452-3906

*PAGE ONE BLACK BOOKS & THINGS, 4732 MALABAR DR., BRUNSWICK, GA 31520...(912) 261-0442

*SHRINE OF THE BLACK MADONNA BOOKSTORE, 946 ABERNATHY BLVD., ATLANTA, GA 30310...(404) 752-6125

*THE DRUM BOOKSTORE, 104 E. BROUGHTON ST., SAVANNAH, GA 31401...(912) 234-9767

*THE KNOWLEDGE TREE, 202 MAIN ST., HINESVILLE GA 31313...(912) 368-8733

HAWAII

*BLACK IMANI BOOKS, 98-027 HEKANA ST. #35, AIEA, HI 96701...(808) 486-5196

ILLINOIS

*AFRICAN AMERICAN BOOK CENTER, 7524 COTTAGE GROVE, CHICAGO,IL 60619...(312) 651-9101

*AFRICAN-AMERICAN IMAGES, 1909 W. 95TH ST. DEPT. SS-5, CHICAGO, IL 60643...

*BLACK HARITAGE BOOKS, 1500 SEWARD ST., EVASTON, IL 60202...(708) 864-0700

* C.O.I. BOOKS & THINGS, P.O. BOX 50035, CICERO, IL 60650...

*C.R.O.E., 2435 W. 71ST ST, CHICAGO, IL 60629 ...(312) 925-1600

*FINAL CALL BOOKS, 734 WEST 79TH ST., CHICAGO, IL 60620...(312) 602-1230

*FREEDOM FOUND BOOKS, 5206 S. HARPER, CHICAGO, IL 60615...(312) 288-2837

*HERITAGE BOOK & MUSIC, 11355 W. GRANVILLE, CHICAGO, IL 60660...(312) 262-1566

*MESSAGE TO THE BLACKMAN INFO. CTR., 4117 W. MADISON, CHICAGO, IL 60624... (312) 722-5111

*WESTSIDE BOOKS, 5941 WEST NORTH AVE., CHICAGO, IL 60639...(312) 288-2837

INDIANA

*ABBA CHRISTIAN BOOKSTORE,3330 N. EMERSON, INDIANAPOLIS, IN 46218...(317) 546-4406

*AFRICAN AMERICAN BOOKS, 3490 VILLAGE CT. GARY, IN 46408...(219) 781-2133

*X-PRESSION,5912 N. COLLEGE AVE., INDIANAPOLIS, IN 46220...(317) 257-5448

*PIC A CARD, 2621 STARDALE, FT. WAYNE IN 46220...(219) 456-6785

IOWA

*UNIVERSITY BOOKSTORE, IOWA M. UNION, IOWA CITY, IOWA 52231...

*AFRICAN CONNECTION, 320 W. KIMBERLY, DAVENPORT, IOWA 52806...(319) 386-4913

KANSAS

*A TOUCH OF HOME, 303 SE 29TH SUITE A, TOPEKA KANSAS 66605...(913) 266-5103

*CULTURAL EXPRESSIONS, 646 STATE AVE., KANSAS CITY, KS 66101...(913) 321-4438,

KENTUCKY

*ALKEBU-LAN IMAGES, LYLES MALL, 2600 BROADWAY, LOUISVILLE, KY 40211...(502) 778-9633

*CARR'S BOOKS, PENNYRILE MALL, HOPKINSVILLE, KY 42240...(502) 886-3330

LOUISIANA

*AUTHENTIC BOOK DISTRIBUTORS, P.O. BOX 52916, BATON ROUGE, LA 70892...(504) 356-0076

*AKBAR'S REST. & BOOKSTORE, 4059 HOLLYWOOD AVE., SHREVEPORT, LA 71109...(318) 621-9993

*BANTU BOOKS, 63 WEST BANK EXPRESSWAY, GRETNA, LA 70053...(504) 362-2688,

*COLLEGIATE BOOKSTORE, 616 HARDING BLVD., BATON ROUGE, LA 70807

*FREEDOM RAGGAE SHOP, 1515 HARDING BLVD., SUITE D, BATON ROUGE, LA 70807...(504) 774-3469

*KENIO'S BOOKS, (HOUSE) 6116 W. UPLAND DR., BATON ROUGE, LA 70811...(504) 356-4269

*KULTURE KORNER, BOX 4296, MONROE, LA 71211...

*REFLECTIONS BOOKS & GIFTS, 9802 HAWTHORN DR., BATON ROUGE, LA 70807...

*SHAKA'S BLACK BOOKSTORE, (HOUSE) 2602 LAKESHORE DR. , SHREVEPORT, LA 71103...(318) 459-2211

*SOUTHERN U. BOOKS,STREET E, BATON ROUGE, LA 70813...(504) 975-5084

MARYLAND

*AFRICAN WORLD BOOKS, 1356 W. NORTH AVE., BALTIMORE MD 21217...(410) 728-0677

*CREATIVE WORKS, 4005 BYERS ST., CAPITAL HEIGHTS, MD 20743...(301) 568-6211

*HERITAGE HEAVEN, 5000 RT. 301 SOUTH, WALDORF, MD 20603...(301) 705-8160

*NUBIAN NETWORK, 3227 CHESTERFIELD AVE., BALTIMORE, MD 21213...(410) 752-1622

*PYRAMID BOOKS, 3062 MONDAWMIN CON, BALTIMORE, MD 21215...(410) 383-8800

MASSACHUSETTS

*AFRO-AMERICAN BOOK SOURCE, P.O. BOX 851, BOSTON, MA 02120...(617) 445-9209,

*AFRO-AMERICAN BOOKSTORE, 872 STATE ST., SPRINGFIELD, MA 01109...(413) 781-2233

*MUHAMMAD'S MOSQUE #11, 417 BLUE HILL, ROXBURY MA 02121...(617) 442-0488

*SAVANNA BOOKS, 858 MASSACHUSETTS AVE., CAMBRIDGE, MA 02139...(617) 868-3423,

*TAPE CONNECTION, 10 WASHINGTON ST., ROXBURY, MASS 02121...(617) 442-0488

MICHIGAN

*AFRICAN CULTURE CON., 2376 STONE DR., ANN ARBOR, MI 48105...(313) 763-3747

*MUHAMMAD MOSQUE BOOKS, 17312 W. 7 MILE, DETROIT, MI 48235...(313) 537-9777

*SHRINE OF THE BLACK MADONNA BOOKSTORE,13535 LIVERNOIS AVE., DETROIT, MI 48238... (313) 491-0777

*STAR RECORDS 45 N. SAGNAW, PONTIAC, MI 48342...(313) 338-3080

*THE BOOK HOUSE INC., 208 W. CHICAGO ST., JONESVILLE, MI 49250...(517) 847-2117

MISSISSIPPI

*HANNAH JOHNSON, 4234 SHERWOOD CIR., MOSS POINT, MS 39563...(601) 475-7272

*JOLOBE BOOKS & THINGS, 914 S. 4TH AVE. LAUREL, MS 36440...

*KAAZIM MUHAMMAD, P.O. BOX 1342, LAUREL, MS 36440...

MISSOURI

*AFROCENTRIC EXPRESSIONS, 7299 OLIVE, ST. LOUIS, MO 63130...(314) 727-9590

*BRANDIES BOOKS & THINGS, 4144 LINDELL, SUITE 102, ST. LOUIS, MO 63108...(314) 534-4324

*ETHIOPIAN OCEAN ART, 1030 BROADWAY, CAPE GIRARDEAU, MO 65701...(314) 334-6499

*FIRST WORLD COLLECTIONS, UNION STATION, 1820 MARKET ST., ST. LOUIS, MO 63103...(314) 421-3433

*GENESIS LTD.,4100 ST. LOUIS AVE, ST. LOUIS, MO 63115...(314) 652-2665

*HIP HOP COMIC BOOK SHOP, 3516 UTAH, ST, LOUIS, MO 63118...(314) 664-0244

*LIL AFRICA, ST. LOUIS CENTRE, 3RD FLR., ST. LOUIS, MO 63101...(314) 621-8180

*PROGRESSIVE EMPORIUM, 6265 DELMAR BLVD., ST. LOUIS, MO 63130...(314) 721-1344

*THE LEARNING CENTER GROUP, 4100 ST. LOUIS AVE., ST. LOUIS, MO 63118...

*UJAMAA UNLIMITED, 4267 MANCHESTER, ST. LOUIS, MO 63110...(314) 535-3238

*W.E.B. DUBOIS LRNG CTR,5501 CLEVELAND AVE., KANSAS CITY, MO 64130...(816) 523-3339

NEBRASKA

*AFRAMERICAN BOOKSTORE,3226 LAKE ST., OMAHA, NE 68111...(402) 455-9200

NEVADA

*** NATIVE SUN**, 1301 D ST., LAS VEGAS, NV 89106...**(702) 647-0101**

NEW MEXICO

***AWAKENING THE NATION**, 225 GARY ST., CLOVIS, NEW MEXICO 88101...**(505) 763-3414**

NEW JERSEY

***HEADSTART ARTS & CRAFTS**, 611 MAIN ST., ASBURY PARK, NJ 07712... **(908) 775-7470,**

***KWANZAA SPECIALTIES**, 91 BUTLEDGE AVE., E. ORANGE, NJ 07017...**(201) 675-6061**

***KNOW YOURSLF BKS & CRAFTS**, P.O. BOX 5819, 160 E. 30TH ST, PATTERSON, NJ 07514

***NEWARK BOOK CENTER**, 10 ACADEMY ST., NEWARK, NJ 07102...**(201) 642-7954**

***QUALITY CUT BARBER SHOP / ISLAMIC STUDY CTR BOOKSTORE**, 1615 MT.EPHRAIM AVE., CAMDEM, NJ 08104... **(609) 365-8148 / (609) 365-0175**

***REJUVENATION HOLISTIC**, 75 CENTRAL AVE., E.ORANGE, NJ 07018...**(201) 672-1220**

***SHABAZZ INTERNATIONAL**, (HOUSE) 469 NORWOOD ST., EAST ORANGE, NJ 07018...(201) 678-7765

*** SHONDOLON BOOKS**, 12 MERCER ST., JERSEY CITY, NJ 07302...**(201) 451-5984**

***TUNDE DADA HOUSE**, 347 MAIN ST., ORANGE, NJ 07050...**(201) 673-4446**, MRS. DADA

NEW YORK

***ISIS & ASSOCIATES**, 260 W. 125TH ST., HARLEM, NY 10027...**(212) 316-3680**

***BLACK BOOKS PLUS**,702 AMSTERDAM AVE., NEW YORK CITY, NY 10025 **(212) 749-9632,**

***BLACK MIND BUILDERS**, 260 W. 125TH ST. MART # 9-A, NEW YORK, NY 10027...**(212) 316-5690**

***BENNU BOOKS**, 656 S. AVE., ROCHESTER, NY 14620...**(716) 271-6810**

***CRESCENT PU. HOUSE**, 103-43 LEFFERTS BLVD., RICHMOND HILL, NY 11411...**(718) 343-8942**

*** FINAL CALL INFO. CTR.**, 1486 FULTON ST., BROOKLYN, NY 11216...**1-800-682-2960**

***HEADSTART BOOKS & CRAFTS, INC.**, 604 FLATBUSH, BROOKLYN, NY 11225...**(718) 469-4500**

***INPUT CULTURE INC.**, 5937 FAUSOLD RD., VALOIS, NY 14888...**(607) 546-6576**

***KAYODE CULTURAL CTR.**, 229-21B MERRICK BLVD., LAURELTON, NY 11413...**(718) 949-5400** OR 5401

***LIBERATION BOOKSTORE INC.**, 421 LENNOX AVE., NEW YORK, NY 10037...**(212) 281-4615**

***MUHAMMAD WISDOM CTR.**, 10141 22 THIRD ST., QUEENSVILLE., NY 11429...**(718) 740-7448**

***NUBIAN PATHWAYS**, 215 CENTRAL AVE., ALBANY, NY 12206...**(518) 463-8673**

***PAN AFRICAN ITERNATIONAL**, 169 BALWIN RD., HEMPSTEAD, NY 11550...**(516) 481-5642**

***POSITIVE IMAGES UNLIMITED BOOKSTORE**, 137-07 BEDELL ST., ROCHDALE VILLAGE, NY11434...**(718) 949-2535**

***POSTERS BY KOLONGI**, P.O. BOX 2348, L.I.C., NY **(718) 545-8750**

***RISING SUN BOOKS**, 378 MARCUS GARVEY BLVD., BROOKLYN, NY 11221...**(718) 571-3901**

***SALAAM TAPE CONNECTION**, 296 LENOX AVE, NEW YORK, NY 10026...**(212) 348-6262**

***SHABAAZ BOOKSTORE**, 102 WEST 116TH ST., NEW YORK, NY 10026...**(212) 749-1889**

***SHAMAL BOOKS INC.**, GPO BOX 2218, NEW YORK, NY 10001...

***THE BLACK BOOK CLUB**, P.O. BOX 40, FANWOOD, NY 07023...**(201) 769-1509,**

***UNIVERSAL BOOKS & RELIGIOUS ARTICLES**, 51 COURT ST., WHITE PLAINS, NY 10601...**(914) 681-0484**

NORTH CAROLINA

***AFRICAN AM ARTS & CRAFTS**, 319 MILBRANCH CIRCLE, GRIFTON, NC 28530...**(919) 524-4922**

***BRISTOL BOOKS**, 3062 120 S. FRONT ST., WILMINGTON, NC 28401...**(919) 251-3770**

***BEACON BOOKSTORE**, 5416 FIELDSTONE DR., RALEEIGH, NC 27609...**(919) 878-7732**

***CLEAN & FRESH PWRHS**, 2405 WEST BLVD., CHARLOTTE, NC 28208...**(704) 37 POWER**

***HALL OF KNOWLEDGE**, 1322 SHAW RD., FAYETTEVILLE, NC 28311...**(919) 630-6040**

***HEADBINDS**, 410 EVANS ST., GREENVILLE, NC 27834...**(919) 758-4516**

***LITTLE PROF. BK CTR.**, LONG LEAF MALL, WILMINGTON, NC 28403...**(710) 395-1378**

***ROOTS CULTURAL**, 612 RED CROSS ST., WILMINGTON,NC 28401...**(919) 763-3972**

***THIRD WORLD BOUTIQUE**, 2904 PATTERSON AVE., WINSTON SALEM, NC 27105...**(919) 722-1119**

***THE HALL OF KNOWLEDGE**, 1322 SHAW RD., FAY, N.C. 28311...**(910) 630-6040**

***UNDERCOVER BOOK SOURCE**, 115 EAST BLVD., CHARLOTTE, NC 28203...

***VENTURA**, 527-D NORTHCHURCH ST., BURLINGTON, NC 27217...**(910) 229-0095**

***YOUR UNDRGRND RL RD**, 209 HENDERSON DR, JACKSONVILLE, NC 28540...**(910) 455-2014**

OKLAHOMA

*S.J. BOOK SHOPPE, 116 N. GREENWOOD, TULSA, OKLAHOMA 74126...(918) 584-7000

OHIO

*ALFATIHA BOOKSTORE, 16 HILLWICK, TOLEDO, OH 43615...(419) 535-9590

*ABDUL'S AFRICAN ARTS, 3956 SALEM AVE., DAYTON, OHIO 45406...(513) 277-6010

*AFRICAN ISLAMIC BOOKS PLUS, 3752 LEE ROAD, SHAKER HEIGHTS, OH 44128...(216) 561-500

*ARTISTIC APPAREL, 730 REDDING RD., CINCINNATI, OH 45237...(513) 361-2787

*CONSCIOUS BOOKS & ETC, 610 GRANT AVE., MATINSFERRY, OH 43935...(614) 635-3142

* ONE NATION BOOKS & ART INC., 1969 DINA CT., POWELL, OH 43065-9020...

*ORIGINAL ARTIFACTS, 1714 N. HIGH ST., COLUMBUS, OHIO 43201...

*RARE BOOKS & THINGS, 1350 LIVINGSTON AVE., COLUMBUS, OH 43205...(614) 258-7576

OREGON

*POWELL'S BOOKS, 1005 WEST BURNSIDE, PORTLAND, OR 97209...(503) 228-0540

PENNSYLVANIA

*CULTURE SHOP, 527 EDGEMONT AVE., CHESTER, PA 19013..(215) 490-0814

*HAKIM'S BOOKSTORE, 210 S. 52ND ST., PHILADELPHIA, PA 19139...(215) 474-9495

*KHALIL'S BOOKS & CULTURE SHOP, 201 E. LINCOLN HWY, COATSVILLE, PA 19320...

*MISCELLANEA LIBRARY, READING TEMNL MKT 12TH & ARCH ST., PHILADELPHIA, PA 19107...(215) 238-9884

*SHAAHID BOOKS & GIFTS, 114 N. MATHILDA ST., PITTSBURGH, PA 15224...(412) 363-3545

*THE AFRO-AMERICAN HISTORICAL AND CULTURAL MUSEUM GIFT SHOP 701 ARCH ST., PHILADELPHIA, PA 19106...(215) 574-3139

*THE TRUTH BOOKSTORE, 104 S. 13TH ST., PHILADELPHIA, PA 19107...(215) 731-1680

RHODE ISLAND

*CORNERSTONE BOOKS, 236 MEETING ST., PROVIDENCE, RI 02906...(401) 331-1340

SOUTH CAROLINA

*DORETHA'S AFR BOOKS, 5410-DTWO NOTCH RD., COLUMBIA, SC 29204...(803) 782-9833

*J&J EXPRESSIONS, 3422 RIVERA AVE., N. CHARLESTON, SC 29406...(803) 782-9833

*RADIANT ALLAH, 3508 CARRIAGE HOUSE LN., COLUMBIA, S.C. 29206...(803) 790-0920

*SALAHUDEEN'S, 108 EAST MAIN ST., BENNETTSVILLE, SC 29512...(803) 579-8842

TENNESSEE

*AFRICAN APPEAL BOOKSTORE, 4011 BRAINERD RD. #B-1, CHATTANOOGA, TN 37411...(615) 624-2318

*ALKEBU-LAN IMAGES, 2721 JEFFERSON ST., NASHVILLE, TN 37208...(615) 321- 4111,

*ARRISE BOOKSTORE, 2531 MLK JR. AVE., KNOXVILLE, TN 37914...(615) 637-1218

*G.S. BOOKS & THINGS, P.O. BOX 231, CORDOVA, TN 38088...

*TWENTY FIRST CENTURY BOOKSTORE, 2027 LAMAR AVE., MEMPHIS, TN 38114...(901) 948-6153

TEXAS

*AFRO AWAKENINGS, 2415 S. COLLINS, ARLINGTON, TX 76014...(817) 265-3053

*AMISTAD BOOKPLACE, 1413 HOLMAN ST., HOUSTON TX 77004...

*BLACK IMAGES BOOK BAZAAR, 142 WYNNEWOOD VILLAGE, DALLAS, TX 75224...(214) 943-0142,

*BLACK VOICES BKSTR, 646 HOLMGREEN, SAN ANTONIO, TX 78220...(210) 333-0118

*BLACKWATCH BOOKS, 2205 JUNIUS ST., SAN ANGELO, TX 76901...(915) 944-8519

*BLACK WORLD BOOKS, 2205 JUNIUS ST., SAN ANTONIO, TX 76901...

*IVORY COAST BOOKS, 303 W. RANCIER AVE. KILLEEN, TX 76541...(817) 634-1511

*KENISE BOOKSTORE, 940 E. BELTLINE RD #164, RICHARDSON, TX 75081...(214) 690-9693

*MULTICULTURE PLUS, 1263 A HIGHWAY 90, LIBERTY, TX 77575...(409) 336-8212

*GOLD'S MUSIC, 3508 N. VERSAILLE, DALLAS, TX 75209...(214) 521-8036

*HERITAGE EXPRESSIONS, 3648 IRVING MALL, IRVING, TX 75062...(214) 255-3890

*HOUSE OF KNOWLEDGE, 1914 DR. MARTIN LUTHER KING BLVD., DALLAS, TX 76522...(214) 421-2818

*NIA GALLERY & BOOKSHOP, HOUSTON, TX...(713) 729-8400

*PAN AFR CONNECTION, 300 S. BECKLEY AVE., DALLLAS, TX 75203...(214) 945-3262

*ROOTS & CULTURE R.B., 3116-B EAST ROSEDALE, FORT WORTH, TX 76105...(817) 534-8495

*SHRINE OF THE BLACK MADONNA BOOKSTORE, 5309 MLK JR. BLVD., HOUSTON, TX 77021...(713) 645-1071

*THE BLACK BOOKWORM BOOKSTORE, 605 E. BERRY ST. SUITE 114, FT. WORTH, TX 76110...(817) 923-9661

*UNDER ONE ROOF, 1539 EAST HIGHWAY 190, COPPERAS COVE, TX 76522...(817) 542-1756

VIRGINIA

*AFRIKA HOUSE, 617 W. 35TH ST., NORFOLK, VA 23508...

*AFRIKA HOUSE OF KNOWLEDGE, 302 E. BROADWAY, HOPEWELL, VA 23860...(804) 723-2696

*BLACKBERRY INC., 1611 S. WALTER REED DR., SUITE 201, ARLINGTON, VA 22204

*CRACKIN' ATOMS, ROUTE 4, BOX 15-A, LOUISA, VA 23093...(703) 894-4872

*ESQUIRE NEWS, 2801 WICKHAM, NEWPORT NEWS, VA 23607

*INCEPTION BOOKSTORE, 7 N. SYCAMORE ST., PETERSBURG, VA 23803...(804) 861-4574,

*IQRAAS BOOKSTORE, 1820 HULL ST., RICHMOND, VA 23224...(804) 737-9641,

*NIA'S BOOKS & THINGS, 9898 LIBERIA AVE., MANASSAS, VA 22110...(703) 369-1412

*POOR BOY MUSIC, 47A FAYETTE ST., MARTINSVILLE, VA 24112...(703) 638-8649

*POSITIVE VIBES, 1025 COMMONWEALTH PL., VA BEACH, VA 23464...

*RESPECT FOR LIFE, 10011-B WEST WASHINGTON ST., PETERSBURG, VA 23803...

*SELF-IMPROVEMENT ED. CTR, 600 WEST 35TH ST., NORFOLK, VA 23508...(804) 623-4910

*SPIRITUALLY UNITED BOOKSTORE, P.O. BOX 36223, RICHMOND, VA 23235...

*TOWNE BOOKS, 2848 JEFFERSON DAVIS #100, STAFFORD, VA 22554...(703) 720-1720

*UB & US BOOKS & THINGS, 912 W. PEMBROKE AVE., HAMPTON, VA 23669...(804) 723-2696

*UJAMAA MART, 103 THIRD ST. N.E., CHARLOTTESVILLE, VA 22902...(804) 977-0921

*YUSUF CONCEPT, 167 D. DELMAR LN., NEWPORT NEWS, VA 23602

WASHINGTON

*BLACKBIRD BOOKS, 313 0 E. MADISON, SEATTLE, WASHINGTON 98112...(206) 325-3793,

*KNOW THYSELF AFRICAN CTR., 1015 S. 12TH ST., TACOMA, WA 98405...(206) 572-8186

WASHINGTON D.C.

*AWA BOOKS AND GIFTS, 2206 18TH ST. NW, WASHINGTON, D.C. 20009...(202) 483-6805

*BLACKBERRY, WASHINGTON, D.C...(703) 486-2297

*HADI COMMUNICATIONS, 2631 JASPER ST. SE #6, WASHINGTON, D.C. 20020...(202) 610-2726

*INSTITUTE FOR HEALING AND HAPPINESS, 3303 11TH ST. NW, WASHINGTON, D.C. 20020...(202) 234-4042

*PYRAMID BOOKSTORE, 2849 GEORGIA AVE. N.W., WASHINGTON, D.C. 20001...(202) 328-0191

*THE AFRICAN EYE, 2134 WISCONSIN AVE. N.W., WASHINGTON, D.C 20007...(202) 625-2552,

*TENTS OF ABRAHAM, 1202 H STREET N.E., WASHINTON, D.C. 20002...

WEST VIRGINIA

*KMT ENTERPRISES, 44 HIGH ST., MORGANTOWN, W. VA 26505

WISCONSIN

*WISCONSIN AFRICAN BOOKS, 3803 W. BURLEIGH ST., MILWAUKEE, WI 53220...(414) 444-7886 OR 444-6605

VIRGIN ISLANDS

*EDUCATION STATION, #20 NISKY CENTER, ST. THOMAS, VI 00802...(807) 776-3008